A New Revelation:
Exploring the Urantia Book

James R. Watkins

CONTENTS

INTRODUCTION

If you gathered the best minds on earth and put them in a room together, and then asked each of them to give their best explanation on how life started, I am convinced no one person could come up with an answer satisfactory to all.

In truth, none of us really knows for sure why we are here. Science may tell us "how" we got here, philosophy and religion can propose "why" we are here, but any explanation is at best, only conjecture.

Much of what I am about to present to you is the result of three decades of careful study and evaluation. Some of what I present will seem outlandish, but I hope it will intrigue you, or will at least get you to consider the possibility there may be forces at work 'behind the scenes,' who are motivated by love and are working on our behalf.

I would like to believe we are not so cynical as to discard anything that doesn't fit into what we would consider to be 'the norm,' and would instead, entertain the possibility that some things *could be true*; that we can still hope and dream about things not yet known, nor yet discovered, for these things are what stir the human soul.

1 CONTACT

It began during the summer of 1911 in an apartment complex located near downtown Chicago. A woman contacted a neighbor, a well-known doctor in the community, to report her husband's strange behavior. The woman told the doctor her husband would move about strangely throughout the night and would remember nothing of what transpired when she questioned him the following morning. When this unusual behavior persisted, the woman, fearing her husband might be suffering from some sort of unusual mental or physical malady, finally decided to call on the doctor who chanced to live nearby for help.

Dr. William S. Sadler was a well-known and accomplished physician in the Chicago area who also lived next door to the couple. Dr. Sadler was contacted on a particular night when the sleeping subject's unusual behavior began to flare up again.

Sadler took on the task of studying and trying to treat the person's behavior, treatment and study that would eventually span *three decades.*

Early accounts by Dr. Sadler state that while observing the strange behavior over a period of several nights, his patient would seemingly move about and sit up during his sleep. At one point the sleeping subject began to communicate to the observing physician - and in a voice *unlike that of the subject.* The conversations, according to Sadler, pertained to subject matter the sleeping subject had no knowledge of, nor was interested in, namely things of a spiritual nature. It was during one particular all-night session Sadler questioned with whom he was speaking.

It was at this time the voice identified himself as a "student visitor."

For long nights over several years these communications continued between the sleeping subject and his supervising physician. The skeptical Dr. Sadler firmly believed the subject suffered some sort of physical or mental disorder, and having earned a reputation of uncovering such claims of channeling or metaphysical exhibitions, his study of this particular patient was fueled almost solely on the desire to explain the phenomena and to find a cure.

Dr. Sadler was extremely skeptical of supposed spiritual or paranormal phenomena during a time when such illusionary displays of "mediumship" (supposed spirits of the deceased speaking through a person) had become quite popular in America. Dr. Sadler was known for his persistent ability to explain apparent psychic phenomena. Sadler would debunk or disprove supposed psychics and mediums, as he firmly believed the human mind could play powerful tricks on unsuspecting or uneducated people. In the field of psychiatrics Dr. Sadler was then considered an early pioneer in the study of mental health, treatment and behavior.

As well versed as he was in explaining supposed paranormal or psychic activity, a frustrated Sadler admitted his own futility and could not explain the unusual behavior displayed by this particular man who talked in his sleep those many nights, months and years under the doctors' careful and skeptical examination.

In an Appendix to his 1929 book *"The Mind at Mischief,"* Dr. Sadler briefly discusses his frustration in not being able to adequately explain this particular case:

"The other exception has to do with a rather peculiar case of psychic phenomena, one which I find myself unable to classify, and which I would like very much to narrate more fully; I cannot do so

here, however, because of a promise which I feel under obligation to keep sacredly. In other words, I have promised not to publish this case during the lifetime of the individual. I hope sometime to secure a modification of that promise and be able to report this case more fully because of its interesting features. I was brought in contact with it, in the summer of 1911, and I have had it under my observation more or less ever since, having been present at probably 250 of the night sessions, many of which have been attended by a stenographer who made voluminous notes.

A thorough study of this case has convinced me that it is not one of ordinary trance. While the sleep seems to be quite of a natural order, it is very profound, and so far we have never been able to awaken the subject when in this state; but the body is never rigid, and the heart action is never modified, tho respiration is sometimes markedly interfered with. This man is utterly unconscious, wholly oblivious to what takes place, and unless told about it subsequently, never knows that he has been used as a sort of clearing house for the coming and going of alleged extra-planetary personalities. In fact, he is more or less indifferent to the whole proceeding, and shows a surprising lack of interest in these affairs as they occur from time to time.

In no way are these night visitations like the séances associated with spiritualism. At no time during the period of eighteen years' observation has there been a communication from any source that claimed to be the spirit of a deceased human being. The communications which have been written, or which we have had the opportunity to hear spoken, are made by a vast order of alleged beings who claim to come from other planets to visit this world, to stop here as student visitors for study and observation when they are en route from one universe to another or from one planet to another. These communications further arise in alleged spiritual beings that purport to have been assigned to this planet for duties of various sorts.

Eighteen years of study and careful investigation have failed to reveal the psychic origin of these messages. I find myself at the present time just where I was when I started. Psychoanalysis, hypnotism, intensive comparison, fails to show that the written or spoken messages of this individual have origin

3

in his own mind. Much of the material secured through this subject is quite contrary to his habits of thought, to the way in which he has been taught, and to his entire philosophy. In fact, of much that we have secured, we have failed to find anything of its nature in existence. Its philosophic content is quite new, and we are unable to find where very much of it has ever found human expression."

It was during these times while treating his subject the Doctor and his wife Lena (also a physician) held informal social weekly meetings in their Chicago home. The Sadler's would regularly entertain friends and fellow members of the community. People from all walks of life would attend these weekly informal gatherings, including prominent business leaders, scholars, farmers, students, fellow doctors and philanthropists, folks who attended the many Sunday gatherings to discuss the news and current events of the day. The gatherings usually numbered between fifty and one hundred people on any given Sunday. Since Dr. Sadler was a well-respected and well-liked member of his community, turnout of these gatherings were always enthusiastic and quite enjoyable social occasions. Each week topics of discussion would include politics, health and medical issues, and on one particular afternoon, a patient that Sadler just couldn't cure.

Sadler, his wife Lena and a fellow doctor who regularly studied the sleeping subject were at a loss to explain the unusual behavior and the in-depth discussions both doctors had been participating in with the patient. To his gathering of friends Sadler described the sessions and how the dialogue of the sleeping subject seemingly came from different individuals, as if multiple personalities were communicating through the patient. Sadler described to some detail the complex and intense theological discussions held between the patient and doctor during those all-night discussions. A stenographer who was always in attendance during these sessions kept notes of these conversations, conversations Sadler said were not the endless ramblings of a madman, nor did they strike Sadler as being coerced philosophic utterances that might lie deep in the subject's sub-conscious seeking to find a way out. The dialogue was consistent and to a large degree, highly intelligent. According to Dr. Sadler, it really was as if a completely different person (or persons) had spoken through the sleeping subject.

Because Sadler had come to know his patient quite well through the years of observing him, he knew his patient neither cared nor did he exhibit much interest in these religious discussions. Sadler stated as a fact that the patient could in no way have had such knowledge of those things conversed between him and the fellow doctors in attendance. And yet, in Sadler's' view there could be no other explanation for such dialogue.

Furthermore, Sadler was intrigued by the depth and scope of knowledge being communicated. It was during one such conversation, said Sadler, the doctor was told by the subject to "take more seriously" what was transpiring and to start asking some "real questions."

Fascinated by Sadler's strange and intriguing story, and in reviewing some of the transcripts of these sessions, his associates beckoned Sadler to let them participate in asking questions and perhaps take up the challenge of the sleeping subject, to which the doctor decided to gather questions and see what would transpire. And so he handed his friends and colleagues 3 x 5 index cards and pencils, instructing them to write down specific question having to do with anything they wanted to know. Sadler even encouraged his associates to ask questions that would be impossible for his patient to answer with any degree of credibility. In this way he could conclusively show the patient was simply displaying some sort of psychological disorder that could be explained.

Sadler sorted out about two hundred separate questions on 3 x 5 index cards, removing multiple or duplicitous questions submitted by his associates on this occasion, and left them in his office safe before retiring for the night. It is said that some weeks later, the patient's wife contacted Dr. Sadler and his wife Lena and urged them to come to the patient's home "as soon as possible." When the two physicians arrived, they were shown a stack of handwritten notes, a rather large volume of papers that had appeared in handwritten form, containing what appeared to be *direct answers* to those very questions submitted by members of the Sadler group some weeks earlier, the same questions he had put in his locked office safe.

Sadler thought that somehow the sleeping subject might be responsible for the writing papers, though how could he have known what to write having not seen any of the questions? However, a handwriting analysis was performed comparing the style of the appearing papers and the style of Dr. Sadler's patient. When compared, the results showed conclusively the patient *did not write the papers*. The patients' wife's handwriting was also checked (because Sadler wanted to make sure every avenue of possibility was explored in order to explain who wrote the initial set of papers). Her handwriting style didn't match either.

In subsequent sessions with the sleeping subject Sadler was told that a "process was being used" by unseen celestial personalities in order to produce the papers and that *no human subject was involved in their formulation*.

Volumes of papers addressing the various questions posed by the group continued to appear from 1925 through 1942, all appearing in handwritten form by an unknown technique that was never revealed in full detail to Dr. Sadler. Sadler would have the penciled notes typewritten and he would give them to members of his group for review. The weekly social meetings became centered on the process of reading and studying what we now know as the *Urantia Papers*; subject matter that described and explained deity, force, energy, cosmology, science, history, philosophy, and religion.

And thus the *Forum* was soon thereafter formed by Sadler; a select group of individuals who would review the papers as they would appear over time. The Forum would continue the process of petitioning new questions. Each week notes from the Forums' sessions would be left in Sadler's locked safe in his study, and then new papers would appear some days later replacing the previous type-written papers. It can be conjectured that the process took place in the following way: whoever wrote the papers would answer the new questions from the group, thus expanding upon the subject matter over time. For years this exchange continued, each time a new set of papers would appear in handwritten form, each time expanding upon the questions and comments submitted by the group who participated in these sessions.

In a personal note written accounting the events years later, Sadler stated that if there were any inconsistencies in the material, then it would have been likely that someone within his group (which eventually numbered over 400 members over time) would have caught it.

No one knows why the communication came about this way or why the authors chose this method. It is commonly believed by many, including Dr. William Sadler, that while this review of the material was taking place, the Forum's reactions played a role in how the celestial agents presented the new and enlarged material. Forum members were reacting to the papers as they read through them, the unseen authors would then add to, or revise some of the information as time went on and as new papers appeared.

From the time the first series of papers appeared until the final papers were received in 1935, a total of 197 separate narratives (or Papers) of subject matter appeared in written form. The total volume of work consisted of 2097 pages of narrative, including the final series of papers containing The Life and Teachings of Jesus, which appeared to everyone's surprise in full volume in 1935.

When no more papers appeared and the type-set work was complete, it is said that Sadler was instructed by the celestial authors in 1942 to begin the preparatory work needed for the eventual publication of the revelatory text. This was reportedly the first time any specific instruction was given regarding publication of the papers. Sadler and his wife Lena then took on the task of raising funds for typesetting and printing the collection of papers. The publication took place in 1955, some twenty years after the final pages appeared, as it required this amount of time to assure all corrections in punctuations, grammar, capitalization and typesetting, including choosing the type of paper, securing the copyright, raising the funds and choosing a printing company.

It is also interesting to point out that the communications between the sleeping subject and Dr. Sadler *stopped abruptly* once publication and printing was complete. Except for a few select people, the identity of the sleeping subject was never revealed, nor was the process of the appearing handwritten papers ever fully explained-even to Sadler himself.

There were no farewells, no final exchanges, except for the final written message from the celestial agents,' which simply said, "You are now on your own."

The sleeping subject resumed his life and no formal contact was ever made again between Sadler and the celestial agents with whom Sadler had maintain almost continual contact for over three decades. All but a few members of the Forum have since passed away, and we may never know why or how the papers appeared, who authored them or be able to verify the source of its contents. Sadler remained skeptical, suspicious and baffled almost to the very end, at which time he "threw in the intellectual towel," and confessed futility as to the process of papers appearing in his locked and secured office. Sadler did confess belief that because of the scope of knowledge needed in order to write the papers, no single human could have contrived them. Sadler went to his grave not knowing for sure, and reluctantly convinced that actual celestial agents could have somehow authored and made material, the Urantia Papers.

And the mystery of how it came to be will ever remain so because the people who were part of its process have long since passed away. In the end, all that remains are documents numbering over two thousand pages. The question of who authored them is shrouded in mystery and is subject to speculation.

Here's what is documented: the book began to surface in the late 20's or 30's and a group of people were involved with the initial study or formulation. We know that Dr. William Sadler told his group that the papers appeared and *he did not know who wrote them*. We also know that for over a three decades, Dr.

Sadler was treating a patient who talked in his sleep and the doctor was instructed by the patient (or whoever was speaking through the patient) to gather up questions and submit them so that answers could be provided. We know that no one (of human origin) to date has claimed authorship; even the copyright of the publication names no author, only a *trustee*. We are left with little information and a group of people who gave testimony that they did not write the papers. To my knowledge, and in my years of research, I have not read, nor have I come across one shred of evidence of anyone coming forth to say "I wrote the book."

With several hundred people involved in the early meetings spanning three decades of time of reviewing the Urantia Papers, surely someone would have spilled the beans by now and claimed responsibility, but such is not the case as far we know.

It is possible that Dr. Sadler would have had the time and the resources to produce the papers, *except for one very important note:* Dr. Sadler was a debunker of strange phenomenon, not a participant. His reputation and credibility were on the line and the possibility of being ostracized or of being exposed (when it could have been easily accomplished by the *mere suggestion* that he played a role) would have been too great. It is simply not likely that a man could have held up a charade for over half a century, especially in the midst of highly intelligent and perceptive members of the community who were witness to the appearance of series of papers, and who later, were involved with their publication.

It would have been the façade of the century, to say the least.

In essence, what the Urantia Papers had to say was ultimately more important to Sadler than who was saying it. And this fact has always been the litmus test of anyone who has perused the documents. It is my contention that for generations to come, the question of *who* wrote the Urantia Papers, instead of *what* was written, will always remain a stumbling block to those people who might otherwise be drawn to its content.

To paraphrase Sadler: if a symphony is beautiful, does it really matter who arranged it?

And so now let us explore the message.

For a more detailed reading on the actual process by which the Urantia papers took place and Dr. Sadler's involvement, I would direct you to an exhaustive account published in 2010. "A History of the Urantia Papers" by Larry Mullins and Dr. Meredith Sprunger."

2 WHO IS GOD AND WHAT IS HE LIKE?

The Urantia Book is presented *as answers* to those questions submitted by the Forum. The first question submitted was, "who is God and what is he like?" Here was their answer, from page 1, paragraph 1 on *The Universal Father*:

"The Universal Father is the God of all creation, the First Source and Center of all things and beings. First think of God as a creator, then as a controller, and lastly as an infinite upholder. The truth about the Universal Father had begun to dawn upon mankind when the prophet said: "You, God, are alone; there is none beside you. You have created the heaven and the heaven of heavens, with all their hosts; you preserve and control them. By the Sons of God were the universes made. The Creator covers himself with light as with a garment and stretches out the heavens as a curtain." Only the concept of the Universal Father — one God in the place of many gods — enabled mortal man to comprehend the Father as divine creator and infinite controller."

The myriads of planetary systems were all made to be eventually inhabited by many different types of intelligent creatures, beings who could know God, receive the divine affection, and love him in return. The universe of universes is the work of God and the dwelling place of his diverse creatures. "God created the heavens and formed the earth; he established the universe and created this world not in vain; he formed it to be inhabited."

11

Remembering that each time Sadler received a new batch of the papers from the unseen authors, they included more information than previously submitted, that is to say, every time a new series of papers "mysteriously appeared," more information would be added on the subject matter being revealed.

The first series of papers to appear had to do with the subject of God, the next time a group of papers appeared, there would be revisions or further clarifications, so that the new series of papers would be provide more detail on the subject matter being presented.

Much of the first series of the Revelation deal specifically with God, energy, force, levels of spirituality, duality of God, the Trinity concept, spiritual personalities who live on high, as well as unknown forces (to man) that operate throughout the universe.

To give you some idea of the scope and subject matter presented in just the first sections of the Urantia Papers (of which there are four complete sections), consider the following titles of the initial ten series of papers presented in written form to Sadler's Forum:

Paper 1 - The Universal Father

Paper 2 - The Nature of God

Paper 3 - The Attributes of God

Paper 4 - God's Relation to the Universe

Paper 5 - God's Relation to the Individual

Paper 6 - The Eternal Son

Paper 7 - Relation of the Eternal Son to the Universe

Paper 8 - The Infinite Spirit

Paper 9 - Relation of the Infinite Spirit to the Universe

Paper 10 - The Paradise Trinity

On the Infinity of God, the author's write:

"Touching the Infinite, we cannot find him out. The divine footsteps are not known." "His understanding is infinite and his greatness is unsearchable. "The blinding light of the Father's presence is such that to his lowly creatures he apparently " dwells in the thick darkness. "Not only are his thoughts and plans unsearchable, but "he does great and marvelous things without number." " God is great; we comprehend him not, neither can the number of his years be searched out." "Will God indeed dwell on the earth? Behold, the heaven (universe) and the heaven of heavens (universe of universes) cannot contain him." "How unsearchable are his judgments and his ways past finding out! "

"There is but one God, the infinite Father, who is also a faithful Creator." "The divine Creator is also the Universal Disposer, the source and destiny of souls. He is the Supreme Soul, the Primal Mind, and the Unlimited Spirit of all creation." "The great Controller makes no mistakes. He is resplendent in majesty and glory." "The Creator God is wholly devoid of fear and enmity. He is immortal, eternal, self-existent, divine, and bountiful " "How pure and beautiful, how deep and unfathomable is the supernal Ancestor of all things!" "The Infinite is most excellent in that he imparts himself to men. He is the beginning and the end, the Father of every good and perfect purpose " "With God all things are possible; the eternal Creator is the cause of causes."

Notwithstanding the infinity of the stupendous manifestations of the Father's eternal and universal personality, he is unqualifiedly self-conscious of both his infinity and eternity; likewise he knows fully his perfection and power. He is the only being in the universe, aside from his divine co-ordinates, who experiences a perfect, proper, and complete appraisal of himself.

The Father constantly and unfailingly meets the need of the differential of demand for himself as it changes from time to time in various sections of his master universe. The great God knows and understands himself; he is infinitely self-conscious of all his primal attributes of perfection. God is not a cosmic accident;

neither is he a universe experimenter. The Universe Sovereigns may engage in adventure; the Constellation Fathers may experiment; the system heads may practice; but the Universal Father sees the end from the beginning, and his divine plan and eternal purpose actually embrace and comprehend all the experiments and all the adventures of all his subordinates in every world, system, and constellation in every universe of his vast domains.

No thing is new to God, and no cosmic event ever comes as a surprise; he inhabits the circle of eternity. He is without beginning or end of days. To God there is no past, present, or future; all time is present at any given moment. He is the great and only I AM." (Paper 2, Section 1, Para. 1-5)

In reading the above, one begins to sense the ring of authenticity on the part of the author; these elaborations on God, being presented to the early Forum for the first time, must have been incredibly impressive.

In summary, the Urantia Book states that of all of the stars we see in our night time sky represent our *superuniverse*, of which there are seven such superuniverses which comprise the *grand universe*; these starry realms are filled with living spiritual and super material beings, along with trillions of planets and solar systems like ours, where material life evolves.

Here is what the authors say about our world, Urantia and its place within the cosmos:

"Your world, Urantia, is one of many similar inhabited planets which comprise the local universe of Nebadon. This universe, together with similar creations, makes up the superuniverse of Orvonton, from whose capital, Uversa, our commission hails. Orvonton is one of the seven evolutionary superuniverses of time and space which circle the never-beginning, never-ending creation of divine perfection — the central universe of Havona. At the heart of this eternal and central universe is the stationary Isle of

Paradise, the geographic center of infinity and the dwelling place of the eternal God."

The seven evolving superuniverses in association with the central and divine universe, we commonly refer to as the grand universe; these are the now organized and inhabited creations. They are all a part of the master universe, which also embraces the uninhabited but mobilizing universes of outer space." (Paper 1, Para. 5, 6)

The Urantia Book describes the first, second and third persons of Deity, **The Trinity** as they relate to all living things:

"The Universal Father is the secret of the reality of personality, the bestowal of personality, and the destiny of personality. The Eternal Son is the absolute personality, the secret of spiritual energy, morontia (ascending) spirits, and perfected spirits. The Conjoint Actor (or Infinite Spirit) is the spirit-mind personality, the source of intelligence, reason, and the universal mind. But the Isle of Paradise is nonpersonal and extra spiritual, being the essence of the universal body, the source and center of physical matter, and the absolute master pattern of universal material reality." (Foreword, Section 8, Para. 5)

"The Paradise Trinity effectively provides for the full expression and perfect revelation of the eternal nature of Deity." (Paper 10, Para. 2)

I have often conjectured on this point by considering the co-existence of these three elements of the universe in the example of the human being. As human beings, we are composed of matter (body), though we function through the will of mind, and we inspired by spirit.

The Revelation states that all things and persons in the universe are responsive to several forms of gravity. In the material world, suns, planets, star systems, interstellar gases, all respond to *physical* gravity. Personality beings are drawn to God (the source of personality) there is a kind of *Mind* gravity which pulls all beings of mind capacity toward the desire for better understanding, knowledge and cooperation. *Spirit* gravity pulls to itself those beings that are striving for spiritual perfection and hunger for spiritual enlightenment – they seek the truth.

In the universe there are *Sons* of God and *Daughters* of the Infinite Spirit, whose role it is to foster new life and oversee the spiritual administration of groups of planets or systems of each inhabited sphere. *Michael* is the name of our Creator Son (we know him as Jesus, but more on that later), *Gabriel* is Michael's assistant, *Immanuel* is also a High Son of God, a Son who actually hails from Paradise and is Michael's spiritual brother. The *Ancients of Days* are a ruling judicial body who hail from *Uversa*, the headquarters of our superuniverse (it is stated the heart of our Milky Way galaxy represents the central region of *Orvonton*, one of seven *super* universes).

Two points of conjecture: Many who are discomfited by such words as *Orvonton*, *Nebadon* and *Urantia*, words that might seem strange, must remember that these words were chosen by the authors as symbols for *the meanings they wanted to convey* (and there was no word in our own language in which to convey them). A closer look at the etymological roots of these words properly discloses their meanings. For example, *Nebadon* might be interpreted as 'city of Nebula,' or 'town of Nebula.' The word *Urantia* might stem from the word *Urania*, which means, 'sky,' or 'among the heavenly place,' and is also represented by the term 'muse of the stars,' found in Greek mythology. It also might stem from the word *Urartu* represents an 'ancient kingdom.' *Ur* is also the oldest known city. So while you and I might find these terms strange, it appears the author's used terminology based on our root Latin and Greek structure in formulating these new words to symbolize these new concepts.

Second, If some of the above names like *Michael*, *Immanuel* and *Gabriel* sound familiar, it might be because these names are littered throughout Scripture:

*"But even the archangel **Michael**, when he was disputing with the devil about the body of Moses, did not himself dare to condemn him for slander but said, "The Lord rebuke you!" - Jude 1:9*

*"I beheld till the thrones were cast down, and the **Ancient of Days** did sit, whose garment was white as snow, and the hair of his head like the pure wool: his throne was like the fiery flame, and his wheels as burning fire."* - Daniel 7:9

*"And he shall pass through Judah; he shall overflow and go over, he shall reach even to the neck; and the stretching out of his wings shall fill the breadth of thy land, O **Immanuel**."* – Isaiah 8:8

*"Yea, whiles I was speaking in prayer, even the man **Gabriel**, whom I had seen in the vision at the beginning, being caused to fly swiftly, touched me about the time of the evening oblation"* – Daniel 9:2

In the spiritual world angels are designated *Seraphim, Supernaphim, Seconaphim, Cherubim* and *Sanobim*, among other names indicative of their spiritual level of existence and descriptive of the duties they perform (more on *angels* in a future chapter). Some types of angelic beings we will never see throughout eternity, others work with us from the time we are born until they day we leave for other heavenly worlds where we find continued learning and progress with and through their assistance:

"Angels do not have material bodies, but they are definite and discrete beings; they are of spirit nature and origin. Though invisible to mortals, they perceive you as you are in the flesh without the aid of transformers or translators; they intellectually understand the mode of mortal life, and they share all of man's non-sensuous emotions and sentiments. They appreciate and greatly enjoy your efforts in music, art, and real humor. They are fully cognizant of your moral struggles and spiritual difficulties. They love human beings, and only good can result from your efforts to understand and love them." (Paper 38, Section 2)

On the universal scale, with God being the highest spiritual being, man stands at the complete opposite end of the spectrum. We are in a sense, a remarkable accomplishment; standing with our feet in two worlds, as we are at the lowest spectrum of the spiritual, and the highest spectrum in the material world. What's more, because God has an actual fragment of his spark *within us,* we are a material form of life *capable of spiritual understanding.*

Accordingly, no other being in the universe will traverse completely from the lowest form of material to the highest estate of spiritual experience, literally with God *within us* throughout the entire journey. We live in Him, and he also lives within us, an actual part of our being. The highest has gone into partnership with the lowest, a partnership that spans an eternity.

The existential Creator meets experiential man and the result is the manifestation of the Father experiencing life through and with his children of time.

The idea of God in partnership with man resonates true. Anyone who has ever loved a child knows that the only thing more thrilling than loving a child is when you know the child innately, without being prompted, loves you in return:

"If the finite mind of man is unable to comprehend how so great and so majestic a God as the Universal Father can descend from his eternal abode in infinite perfection to fraternize with the individual human creature, then must such a finite intellect rest assurance of divine fellowship upon the truth of the fact that an actual fragment of the living God resides within the intellect of every normal-minded and morally conscious Urantia mortal..."

"...Man does not have to go farther than his own inner experience of the soul's contemplation of this spiritual-reality presence to find God and attempt communion with him." (Paper 5, Section 1)

The Revelators are emphatic:

"Mortal man is not an evolutionary accident. There is a precise system, a universal law, which determines the unfolding of the planetary life plan on the spheres of space." (Paper 49, Section 1)

Are you now starting to get a sense of the depth and scope of the information being put forth? Are you starting to understand how exhaustive such a narrative could possibly be, and the preposterousness that someone or a group of people would go to such great lengths to *make it all up* as a fanciful attempt to create a fictional account of reality?

Remember that members of the Forum, upon reading these concepts for the first time, must have been amazed by the depth of spiritual concepts being presented.

If the Revelators seek to accomplish anything, it is perhaps for us to conceptualize the great universal effort and intelligence involved in the progressive development of our cosmos. In the Urantia Book man is no longer just a struggling or unimportant being, but rather a mortal being driven to make a better life for himself, a more perfect world in which to live and grow.

The driving force is twofold; man wants comfort, and he wants safety. The spiritual forces behind the scenes urge him to find both for the purpose of allowing man eventually to have both comfort and safety - and then begin to contemplate the higher realities of existence – *his actual spiritual destiny.*

A hungry man has little time to ruminate on the value of his place in the universe, but a society of comfortable men now have leisure to contemplate the values and meanings of universal progress which strives for and attains eventual perfection:

"The fact of animal evolutionary origin does not attach stigma to any personality in the sight of the universe as that is the exclusive method of producing one of the two basic types of finite intelligent will creatures. When the heights of perfection and eternity are attained, all the more honor to those who began at the bottom and joyfully climbed the ladder of life, round by round, and who, when they do reach the heights of glory, will have gained a personal experience which embodies an actual knowledge of every phase of life from the bottom to the top."

"In all this is shown the wisdom of the Creators. It would be just as easy for the Universal Father to make all mortals perfect beings, to impart perfection by his divine word. But that would

deprive them of the wonderful experience of the adventure and training associated with the long and gradual inward climb, an experience to be had only by those who are so fortunate as to begin at the very bottom of living existence." (Paper 32, Section 3)

3 THE LIVING UNIVERSE

"Our Earth is one of millions of inhabited spheres that compose an almost limitless universe," so says the Revelation.

There are literally thousands of statements contained within the writings of the Revelation that paint a picture of a functional, operational and intelligently controlled universe, administered by super-material beings of a divine or deified nature.

Consider the following unique concepts presented in the narrative:

❑ God the Father is a *real personality* and the First Source and Center of all things; we are his ascendant children of time and space

❑ The universe is filled with various types of *"Sons"* of God who administer to and are responsible for the various creations of planets and life on those planets throughout the far-flung universes

❑ Man is evolutionary, his destiny is spiritual because he contains spiritual potential, *an actual soul*

❑ There are hundreds of millions of evolutionary worlds; these worlds produce various types of material beings of spirit capacity who, upon physical death, begin an ascendant journey which leads towards the Universal

Father of all creation, who resides on Paradise, the geographical center of seven superuniverses

- Spiritual forces and personalities *intelligently* guide evolution. Angels and other types of high spiritual personalities will become more evident to us in the next life, but they do assist us in the material existence

- Adam and Eve were **divine** beings who lived among us 39,000 years ago in an area along the Eastern Mediterranean shores, and later, relocated to what is now Iraq. There, they founded a superior civilization

- Jesus was and is the literal *Creator Son* of our Universe. He chose our world for his seventh and final bestowal to gain experience as a mortal man and to teach a further revelation of God to men

- Machiventa Melchizedek, a divine Son (known biblically as the "Sage of Salem") taught Abraham the one-God concept which was the basis of Judaism. It was this Sons' emergency efforts 4,000 years ago (around 1,997 B.C.) that prevented the one-God concept from vanishing completely from the human race. Melchizedek revealed further truth to mankind and through the efforts of this Son's missionaries, were able to spread his doctrine, now found in almost every major religion in the world

- It is the Universal plan that all evolutionary worlds eventually attain spiritual enlightenment

- The Urantia Book was given to us to fill in the missing gaps of our early history, and to afford mankind a clarified explanation of who we are, how we came to be and what our global - as well as spiritual destiny is in the ages to come

- ❏ Our world Urantia is "out of step," with normal evolutionary worlds due to the default of Adam and Eve 39,000 years ago, and prior to that, the Lucifer Rebellion which had an effect on our early cultures some 250,000 years ago; this latest Revelation is an attempt to correct these mishaps and bring about a new awareness of our spiritual destiny as evolutionary mortals of spiritual destiny

- ❏ Lucifer did rebel against the rulers of the Universe some 250,000 years ago. Remnants of this event are found in our Scriptural records, though in distorted form. The Urantia Book presents a detailed account of this event

- ❏ There is an actual and definite life beyond our mortal death, and this spiritual life in "Heaven" is explained in full detail

The Revelation is comprised of four parts, with the fourth part an exhaustive account of the Life and Teachings of Jesus, including a comprehensive narrative of Jesus' childhood, his later travels and days as a teacher among men in and around Palestine and the Mediterranean some two-thousand years ago.

The four sections of the Revelation narrate the following subject matter:

- **The Central Universe** and the personalities who are charged with its administration, this encompasses the Origin and Nature of God, the Three Persons of the Trinity, the various forms of known energy and the physical aspects of the grand universe

- The second part is a narrative of the personalities and physical aspects of **The Local Universe**; a local universe consists of upwards to 10 million worlds, our local universe is called **Nebadon**.

- ***The History of Our World (Urantia)***; These series of papers deal with the chronological history of our world, from the creation of our solar system, on down through the various planetary stages of evolutionary life, the emergence of a mammal of will status and early societal development up to about the time when our own written records began to appear

- ***The Life and Teachings of Jesus***. Here, the narrative provides 800 pages of almost every facet of the life of Jesus. The Revelators claim the reason for the presentation was to provide a full account of the life of the Creator Son, as he lived it on earth. The narrative covers his birth, the stories of Joseph and Mary, the life of John the Baptist, the apostles and the general circumstances of Jesus' life as he lived it in Palestine and his travels around the Roman Empire prior to his public life as a preacher and healer. The presentation also details the crucifixion; his appearances after his mortal death and how the early disciples went on to form the early Christian Church

The first section of the Urantia Book reads more like a theological instruction manual as it seeks to present new and complex concepts having to do with the varying natures of Deity, also of divinity, force and energy. The authors needed us to learn a new language so that concepts appearing later in the book would make more sense.

The Revelators make a point of explaining why they choose to start with the most complex concepts first:

*"The human mind would ordinarily crave to approach the cosmic philosophy portrayed in these revelations by proceeding from the simple and the finite to the **complex** and the infinite, from human origins to divine destinies. But that path does not lead to spiritual wisdom. Such a procedure is the easiest path to a certain form of genetic knowledge, but at best it can only reveal man's origin; it reveals little or nothing about his divine destiny."*

Also, on how starting with origins *first* helps present a more complete picture of reality:

"The true perspective of any reality problem--human or divine, terrestrial or cosmic--can be had only by the full and unprejudiced study and correlation of three phases of universe reality: origin, history, and destiny. The proper understanding of these three experiential realities affords the basis for a wise estimate of the current status." (Paper 19, Section 1, Para. 5, 6)

In this way, when man knows where he came from, where he is going and why, so does he better understand the *wisdom* of this ascension plan as it is laid out before him. The method of starting with *origins first* helps us gain a truer understanding of our destiny.

For the purposes of making sure we have an accurate presentation, even at the risk of initial rejection from most who might peruse the Urantia Book for the first time and be put off by its initial complex description of God and reality, still the Revelators thought it best to start at the top and work their way down. This method was intended to build a foundation of overall understanding.

For the first time a clear-cut picture of *what does exist beyond the grave of mortality* is presented in full detail. The authors sought to leave no stone unturned in telling us exactly how the structure of life is set up, and exactly what our roles in it are as we take this first step of a long, long, journey.

The various Sons of God are manifestations of the varying natures of God, personal representatives of Gods' eternal being. These *Sons* of God carry out the mandate and administrative duties of the *Eternal Son* – the *Second Person* of the Trinity.

Spirit personalities (angels, cherubim's, seraphim, etc.) are *offspring* of the Infinite Spirit – the *Third Person* of the Trinity - offspring in that they are representative of the Spirits' mission of progressive ascension and loving administration. Spirits are real beings who possess real forms and are real personalities who find their origin in the Infinite Spirit.

The symmetry of the Trinity *is the very relationship* that spawns life and provides the ongoing dynamic expression that provokes growth through the living universe. Just as we raise children through trial, error, so does God, his Son together with the Infinite Spirit raise entire universe families of spiritual children, who in turn assist in the guidance of the children of men through spirit guidance.

That the comment made to Sadler, "why don't you start asking some real questions," would result in highly complex descriptions of Deity itself must have proven somewhat bewildering to Sadler and his associates. In a sense, they were going to school; they were being introduced to never-before and advanced spiritual concepts. It made current theology seem almost like a Dr. Seuss book. The papers presented a reality much more intricate and *organized.*

Here is how the Revelators describe the physical Grand Universe: From the Central Universe of *Havona* (which is a never beginning and never ending universe which encircles Paradise), there are seven super universes. Within each superuniverse there are 1 trillion potential worlds for inhabitants. Each superuniverse is comprised of sectors, constellations and systems. Each local system contains potentially a thousand inhabited worlds (our world is the 606th evolved sphere of human life and is called *Urantia*).

Some inhabitable worlds are located in solar systems with one star, other worlds that might harbor life may be earth-sized satellites circling large planets and receive enough light and heat from the central orb as well as the lager sphere they may be encircling. Most evolutionary worlds produce mammalian types of creatures, but no two worlds are exactly the same; all inhabited worlds produce distinctively different racial types, and all worlds are under the watch care of spiritual forces. *We are not accidents in time.* Our world, like others, was planned.

The book addresses this challenge of presenting new truth to mankind:

"We are fully cognizant of the difficulties of our assignment; we recognize the impossibility of fully translating the language of the concepts of divinity and eternity into the symbols of the language of the finite concepts of the mortal mind. But we know that there dwells within the human mind a fragment of God and that there sojourns with the human soul the Spirit of Truth; and we further know that these spirit forces conspire to enable material man to grasp the reality of spiritual values and to comprehend the philosophy of universe meanings. But even more certainly we know that these spirits of the Divine Presence are able to assist man in the spiritual appropriation of all truth contributory to the enhancement of the ever-progressing reality of personal religious experience — God-consciousness." (Foreword, Section 12)"

Revelation of *new truth* is necessary for man to grow:

"Revelation is evolutionary but always progressive. Down through the ages of a world's history, the revelations of religion are ever-expanding and successively more enlightening. It is the mission of revelation to sort and censor the successive religions of evolution. But if revelation is to exalt and up step the religions of evolution, then must such divine visitations portray teachings which are not too far removed from the thought and reactions of the age in which they are presented. Thus must and does revelation always keep in touch with evolution. Always must the religion of revelation be limited by man's capacity of receptivity.

"But regardless of apparent connection or derivation, the religions of revelation are always characterized by a belief in some Deity of final value and in some concept of the survival of personality identity after death."

"Evolutionary religion is sentimental, not logical. It is man's reaction to belief in a hypothetical ghost-spirit world — the human belief-reflex, excited by the realization and fear of the unknown. Revelatory religion is propounded by the real spiritual

*world; it is the response of the super intellectual cosmos to the mortal hunger to believe in, and depend upon, the universal Deities. Evolutionary religion pictures the circuitous groping's of humanity in quest of truth; revelatory religion is **that very truth**."* (Paper 92, Section 4, Para 1, 2, 3)

And on the Urantia Papers being the most recent revelation of revealed truth to mankind:

"The Urantia Papers." The papers, of which this is one, constitute the most recent presentation of truth to the mortals of Urantia. These papers differ from all previous revelations, for they are not the work of a single universe personality but a composite presentation by many beings. But no revelation short of the attainment of the Universal Father can ever be complete. All other celestial ministrations are no more than partial, transient, and practically adapted to local conditions in time and space. While such admissions as this may possibly detract from the immediate force and authority of all revelations, the time has arrived on Urantia when it is advisable to make such frank statements, even at the risk of weakening the future influence and authority of this, the most recent of the revelations of truth to the mortal races of Urantia." (Paper 42, Section 4, Para.9)

Ultimately, it is the reader has to decide, without fanfare or ceremonial practice, whether the author's revelations ring true, just as did the Forum and Dr. Sadler had to decide when they were first being presented the material. Man naturally likes his religion to be colorful and magical. For this reason so many religions have remained. Man likes to believe in something mysterious, and the only thing mysterious about the Urantia Book is that it claims to be from *the spiritual world*, from the very personalities with whom we will greet in the life to come.

But is there proof to such claims? Let us examine of few of them.

4 CLUES OF VERIFICATION

The subject invariably always comes up among readers "what makes you think the Urantia Book is authentic, or even credible?"

There is one story I can share about a man who discovered the papers sometime after they were first published in 1955. This gentleman is Meredith Sprunger, a United Church of Christ Minister in Ft. Wayne, Indiana, who once recounted how a friend gave him a copy of the book and asked if he would provide his opinion as to the books' authenticity.

After some light reading, the minister says he initially thought much of what the book had to say seemed pretentious and fictional (his exact words were 'gobbeldy-gook'). The minister was impressed by its great detail, but was confounded by why anyone would waste his or her time with such a large volume of seemingly useless 'metaphysical nonsense.'

After some initial hesitation, the minister gave it one more shot (feeling he owed his friend at least an educated response), and so on one evening, while he had some spare time, he sat down and chose to read a series of chapters entitled, "The Life and Teachings of Jesus."

Meredith, being of clergy, was captivated by the title and felt he would at least be somewhat interested in what these strange papers might have to say about Jesus. It was at this pivotal moment, as this learned man of Scripture stated the rich detail of Jesus' life "jumped out at him." After months of prior - even uninteresting casual reading- suddenly the import of the papers began to take on a more impressive tone. Dr. Meredith Sprunger recognized his *clues of verification*, as he says they were so eloquently portrayed on the pages of the Revelation, and "rang with the recognition of truth."

The Minister, since that day, has become not just a reader, but also a key figure and supporter in the blending of biblical teachings as well as the Urantia Papers he so easily tried to discard some forty-years prior. As a minister he came to understand (and believe) the papers to be credible, original and authentic. To this day the papers remain an integral part of his ministry.

I personally spoke with Dr. Sprunger on three occasions and asked him what changed his mind, what made him believe in the authenticity of the Urantia Book, or at least in the section having to do with Jesus's life and teachings. He said he was convinced of the Revelations' authenticity after studying the section of the papers that detail the lives of the twelve Apostles. Sprunger was quoted later as stating, "No one could have put forth such convincingly true description of their personalities unless they knew what they were talking about." He added "unless you knew them personally, you could not have portrayed them with such a clear understanding."

The following selected story of the Apostle Thomas illustrates the rich detail of the writings found in the Jesus Papers:

"The early home life of Thomas had been unfortunate; his parents were not altogether happy in their married life, and this was reflected in Thomas's adult experience. He grew up having a very disagreeable and quarrelsome disposition. Even his wife was glad to see him join the apostles; she was relieved by the thought that her pessimistic husband would be away from home most of the time. Thomas also had a streak of suspicion which made it very difficult to get along peaceably with him. Peter was very much upset by Thomas at first, complaining to his brother, Andrew, that

Thomas was "mean, ugly, and always suspicious." But the better his associates knew Thomas, the more they liked him. They found he was superbly honest and unflinchingly loyal. He was perfectly sincere and unquestionably truthful, but he was a natural-born faultfinder and had grown up to become a real pessimist. His analytical mind had become cursed with suspicion. He was rapidly losing faith in his fellow men when he became associated with the twelve and thus came in contact with the noble character of Jesus. This association with the Master began at once to transform Thomas's whole disposition and to effect great changes in his mental reactions to his fellow men.

Thomas's great strength was his superb analytical mind coupled with his unflinching courage — when he had once made up his mind. His great weakness was his suspicious doubting, which he never fully overcame throughout his whole lifetime in the flesh.

In the organization of the twelve Thomas was assigned to arrange and manage the itinerary, and he was an able director of the work and movements of the apostolic corps. He was a good executive, an excellent businessman, but he was handicapped by his many moods; he was one man one day and another man the next. He was inclined toward melancholic brooding when he joined the apostles, but contact with Jesus and the apostles largely cured him of this morbid introspection.

Jesus enjoyed Thomas very much and had many long, personal talks with him. His presence among the apostles was a great comfort to all honest doubters and encouraged many troubled minds to come into the kingdom, even if they could not wholly understand everything about the spiritual and philosophic phases of the teachings of Jesus. Thomas's membership in the twelve was a standing declaration that Jesus loved even honest doubters." (Paper 139, Section 8, Para. 3-6)

The papers describing the twelve Apostles within the context of Jesus' life are but one example of the transforming effect the papers have had on many scholars. Sadler himself said the papers describing the personalities of the Apostles convinced him as well that whoever wrote the papers almost seemed to have been there in person, or had incredible information from which to go on.

Here is another example, having to do with Jesus Apostles' Andrew and Peter:

"Andrew and Peter were very unlike in character and temperament, but it must be recorded everlastingly to their credit that they got along together splendidly. Andrew was never jealous of Peter's oratorical ability. Not often will an older man of Andrew's type be observed exerting such a profound influence over a younger and talented brother. Andrew and Peter never seemed to be in the least jealous of each other's abilities or achievements. Late on the evening of the day of Pentecost, when, largely through the energetic and inspiring preaching of Peter, two thousand souls were added to the kingdom, Andrew said to his brother: "I could not do that, but I am glad I have a brother who could." To which Peter replied: "And but for your bringing me to the Master and by your steadfastness keeping me with him, I should not have been here to do this." Andrew and Peter were the exceptions to the rule, proving that even brothers can live together peaceably and work together effectively." (Paper 139, Section 1, Para. 6)

Many individuals who have perused the papers find it difficult at first to accept the notion that such an authoritative book could contain factual information on the origins of God or of spiritual beings co-existing in the material realm, or even the factual day-by-day accounts of Jesus. At first glance, one would be hard pressed to believe any person could be credibly and factually accurate in writing about the subject matter outlined above. A brilliant writer could very easily compose fantastic fiction, and of course, none of it could be real. Great fantasy has been written, believable as anything contained in the Revelation.

And then there are specific details contained within the Revelation not previously known.

Let me illustrate one item that is written about the *Star of Bethlehem*, the star depicted in almost all scenes of the baby

Jesus in the manger, the guiding star that led the three wise men from the East to Bethlehem on the night of Jesus' birth:

The Revelators state that Jesus was actually born at noon on August 21, 7 B.C, owing to the later revision of the Julian calendar, the actual birth of record dated back from the writings of the Revelation, is said to be 7 B.C. Historians may be able to confirm this, but for the point of my illustration, let us assume that the author is correct on the date, and further point out an astonishing statement contained in the text of the papers.

The narrative points out that three times during the year Jesus was born, a planetary conjunction occurred with Jupiter and Saturn in the Constellation of Pisces. This astronomical event is stated to have happened on May 29th, September 29th and December 5th of that year. Because of the proclivity of men to mix facts with miracles, the legend of a bright evening star appearing as a guiding light to herald the miraculous birth of Jesus was later interwoven in the biblical account, so says the Revelation. But it is of astronomic record that this brilliant conjunction occurred at about the same period of time of Jesus' birth, and legend sprang from these two separate, but wholly natural events.

This was an amazing statement. In all of my years of Christian upbringing, no one ever correlated the Star of Bethlehem with a planetary conjunction. Most of us accept the Star of Bethlehem as either a nice piece of biblical fantasy or an actual miracle without question. Years later, somewhat curious as to whether or not this statement could be proven, I turned on my computer, loaded an astronomy software program, entered the dates of *May 29th*, *September 29th*, and *December 5th*. I entered the location of Bethlehem and surprisingly, the facts turned out to be true that in 7 B.C., a conjunction did occur exactly as stated in the narrative of the Revelation.

I then contacted the Lowell Observatory in Flagstaff, Arizona and asked an astronomy instructor if they had heard of, or was it of any significance that a planetary conjunction of this sort occurred in the year 7 B.C. The astronomer said he could not recall those dates as being significant. I also asked if it was possible for astronomers to track star courses and planetary conjunctions with great accuracy prior to 1935 (the year the papers were written). The observatory official and resident astronomer said that it was possible, but only major events prior to 1600 A.D. such as recurring comets or stellar explosions, etc., were likely to get any attention.

Pushing further, I asked the Lowell Observatory astronomer if it was possible an astronomer in 1935 could have done his research and discovered the conjunction of 7 B.C. and tied it in to the Star of Bethlehem. Prior to the 1930's, I asked, could anyone other than a highly educated astronomer know that in the year 7 B.C, a conjunction of Jupiter and Saturn occurred in the Constellation of Pisces on the exact dates mentioned? He said he would look into it and would get back with me. Three days later I received an email from my contact stating that there was "no known record of this conjunction as being a significant astronomical event, and unless someone was specifically looking for it, it would be largely overlooked by the astronomy community."

In other words, the author of the Urantia Book was either extremely lucky to have picked three random dates, chose two random planets in our solar system, and accurately correlated them with an event we have come to know as the Heralding of the Birth of Christ, or the author had information even esteemed astronomers did not have access to until the advent of computer software programs would arrive some 60 years later.

And then there's the clarification of a supposed miracle. Why would someone want to clear up a misconception of a supposed miraculous event when in doing so, the only result would be to diminish the importance of the event itself? Could it be the authors' intent was to provide **truth** in the place of **error**? Could it be the authors' intent was to provide clues of verification for those future readers?

In my view, it was a respectable way to provide "revealed" truth, without calling too much attention to it. Rather casually, the author provides information that no one could have possibly known in 1935:

"The beautiful legend of the star of Bethlehem originated in this way: Jesus was born August 21 at noon, 7 B.C. On May 29, 7 B.C., there occurred an extraordinary conjunction of Jupiter and Saturn in the constellation of Pisces. And it is a remarkable astronomic fact that similar conjunctions occurred on September 29 and December 5 of the same year. Upon the basis of these extraordinary but wholly natural events the well-meaning zealots of the succeeding generation constructed the appealing legend of the star of Bethlehem and the adoring Magi led thereby to the manager, where they beheld and worshiped the newborn babe. Oriental and near-Oriental minds delight in fairy stories, and they are continually spinning such beautiful myths about the lives of their religious leaders and political heroes. In the absence of printing, when most human knowledge was passed by word of mouth from one generation to another, it was very easy for myths to become traditions and for traditions eventually to become accepted as facts." (Paper 122, Section 8, Para. 7)

Nativity scenes have never looked the same since:

Another clue of verification discovered most recently was what the Revelators have to say Neanderthal man. Compare two passages, one from an article by Joe Alper in the June 2003 *Smithsonian Magazine* on recent discoveries of Neanderthal artifacts in France and parts of southern Europe:

For a longtime, Paleontologists have viewed Neanderthals as too dull and too clumsy to use efficient tools, never mind whether they could organize a hunt and divvy up game. Recent studies suggest they were imaginative enough to carve artful objects and perhaps clever enough to invent a language.

Alper continues:

Researchers now believe (because of new discoveries) they were highly intelligent, able to adapt to a wide variety of ecological zones and capable of developing highly functional tools to help them do so. They were quite accomplished.

Alper mentions some of the tools found at the archeological digs include reindeer bones etched into carving tools, and makeshift graves indicative of the Neanderthal burying their dead-a custom never before attributed to the Neanderthal race.

In 1934, the following passages appear in the Revelatory text on the subject of Neanderthals:

"The Neanderthalers were excellent fighters, and they traveled extensively. They gradually spread from the highland centers in northwest India to France on the west, China on the east, and even down into northern Africa."

Regarding the use of tools and customs, the Revelators state:

"The reindeer was highly useful to these Neanderthal peoples, serving as food, clothing, and for tools, since they made various uses of the horns and bones...Large flints attached to wooden handles came back into use and served as axes and picks."

Notice the similarity of Joe Alpers' article to that of the Revelation:

"Other tools (found) would have been hafted or set in wooden handles...recovered stone tools typically fashioned from nearby sources of flint or quartz."

And that in the year 2003, researchers believed:

"Neanderthal groups mingled and exchanged mates; such interactions may have been necessary for survival."

When, in 1934, the Revelators state *with authority*:

"...Neanderthalers were the first to adopt the practice of giving the most successful hunters the choice of women for wives."

The point here is this: How is it the author's in 1934 had more information about an extinct species than paleontologists did in the year 2003? There are three possible answers, they either guessed, they had information which hadn't been released to the scientific community, or, as they claim, they were there.

Clues of verification are to be found throughout the revelatory text. The aforementioned examples are illustrative of how the Revelators chose to provide insight into man's distant and often misconstrued past.

When paleontologists recently herald the confirmed theory of birds evolving from the reptile family, the Revelators had already stated it as fact some 60 years previous:

"55,000,000 years ago the evolutionary march was marked by the sudden appearance of the first of the true birds, a small pigeon like creature which was the ancestor of all bird life. This was the third type of flying creature to appear on earth, and it sprang directly from the reptilian group."

Again indicative that whoever authored the papers knew very much about things we have only recently discovered in science, health and human history. As more people find the Revelation and peruse its volumes of data, no doubt more clues of verification will surface.

Several years ago a very brilliant and astute Urantia Book reader compiled a short list of statements made in the text of the Revelation that turned out later to be verified by science. Philip Calabrese listed his own clues of verification – positions either taken or revealed for the first time in the Urantia Book.

Calabrese writes:

"The following are implausible scientific positions and predictions that are now accepted by contemporary scientists (but weren't at the time of the Urantia Books publication in 1955):

1) *"Piltdown Man"* - *The 1912 & 1917 "missing link" fossils, a hoax finally exposed and discredited after 1950. Almost all scientists in the field were fooled including William Gregory and Henry Osborn. Had (the Urantia Book) taken "Piltdown Man" seriously The Urantia Book would have discredited itself as a divine revelation. But while acknowledging and describing Neanderthal, Cro-Magnon, Java and Heidelberg man, and even while affirming evolutionary theory's main lines of thought, The Urantia Book nevertheless flatly states that no such "missing link" (aka "Piltdown Man") will be found because none exists [p.669]. Conservatively, less than 2% of scientists disbelieved Piltdown "missing link" man. The probability of randomly choosing these over the others is less than 1 in 50.*

2) **Pangaea** - *Alfred Wegener's 1920's theory of a single continent that broke apart and "drifted" (largely rejected by 1929, vindicated in the late1950's and 60's). Continents float on liquid rock; allowed "continental drift". Only a few geologists defended Wegener's theory of continental drift until the 1950's. So the probability of randomly choosing their position is less than 1 in 20. But the UB embraces it. [p.663]*

3) **Plate Tectonics**. *Collisions of continents with obstructions cause mountains; shifting now causes earthquakes; periodic submergence continues. [p.688-9] Since these were not the expressed positions of most contemporary scientists, the probability of randomly choosing these positions is rather generously estimated to be as much as 1 in 2.*

4) **Injury Repair Cell Proliferation**. *As late as 2001 Dr. Emilio Orfei, Department of Pathology, Loyola University of Chicago, wrote that the injury response is still not understood and may be humoral, something the Urantia Book said in 1955. [UB, p.735] A correct description of this injury repair mechanism was unknown in 1955. The probability that some correct human description written before 1955 was somehow chosen by human authors of the UB is generously estimated to be as much as 1 in 50.*

5) ***Hundreds of Millions of Galaxies***. *New cosmic maps of the whole universe are now confirming the bold cosmic predictions made by the Urantia Book before 1955: "No less than 375 million" galaxies in far outer space. [p.130] only in the 1990's did our scientists confirm what the Urantia Book said in 1955. Large scale ring structures separated by "voids" predicted to circle in the plane of the Milky Way. [p.125] The probability of there being some correct human description before 1955 which somehow was chosen by human authors is generously estimated at less than 1 in 100th of a chance.*

6) ***Large scale structures in the universe***. *In the 1980's, expecting randomness astronomers were surprised to see "large scale structures", "walls of galaxies", separated by huge voids, walls that may circle the Local Group (Grand Universe) including the Milky Way (Orvonton). [UB,p.129]. No prominent astronomers were predicting non-randomly spaced galaxies in far outer space. The probability of human authors correctly guessing this is again generously estimated to be no more than 1 in 100.*

7) ***Huge Redshifts***. *Before they were observed, the Urantia Book predicted huge redshifts equivalent to recessional speeds of "more than thirty thousand miles a second", (but it also instructs that this does not mean the universe is flying apart) [p.134]. In data provided by Allan Sandage at Mt. Wilson and Las Campanas Observatories the Hydra galaxy is now estimated to have a recessional speed of 61,000 km/sec = (61,000 /1.609) miles/sec = 37,900 miles/sec, which would be more than 1/5 the speed of light! Although Hubble discovered that the amount of redshift is linearly related to distance, such large redshifts as described by the UB were not seen until new telescopes revealed them, just as the UB predicted. Few if any scientists were predicting such large redshifts would soon be seen with better telescopes. They might have been wondering. The Urantia Book flatly makes a quantitatively accurate prediction even while disputing the predictable interpretation of such huge red shifts as supposedly indicating an explosive "big bang" occurred. Estimated probability of human authors making the prediction is no more than 1 in 5.*

*8) **Dark Matter Holds the Universe Together**. That dark matter holds luminous bodies together was first noticed in 1970's. Wikipedia, the free encyclopedia tells us, "In the 1970s it was realized that the total visible mass of galaxies (from stars and gas) does not properly account for the speed of the rotating gas, thus leading to the postulation of dark matter." But The UB said this already in 1955. [p.173] the probability of human authors taking this position is very generously estimated to be as much as 1 in 5. Actually, very few if any scientists were saying anything like this back in 1955.*

*9) **Neutrinos**. While W. Pauli predicted neutrinos in 1931 and E. Fermi incorporated them into his 1934 theory of atomic decay, they were not actually observed until 1959. But The Urantia Book boldly affirms their existence as "certain small uncharged particles", describes their role [p.479], and says all such particles respond to gravity (have mass) [p.461]. But only in 1998 did our scientists discover that neutrinos have mass, and it has upset their "Standard Theory". Estimated probability of human authors taking these correct positions is again very generously assigned the value 1 in 4.*

According to Calabrese, The Urantia Book statements were ahead of science in stating as fact what was only known to be theory or conjecture in 1955, the year the Urantia Book was published.

Since 1955 the book has been in existence for all to read. Thus far most of the claims it makes that can be proven have been, and the clues to verification of its authenticity continue to grow.

5 HUMAN LIFE BEGINS

"From the year A.D. 1934 back to the birth of the first two human beings is just 993,419 years.

These two remarkable creatures were true human beings. They possessed perfect human thumbs, as had many of their ancestors, while they had just as perfect feet as the present-day human races. They were walkers and runners, not climbers; the grasping function of the big toe was absent, completely absent. When danger drove them to the treetops, they climbed just like the humans of today would. They would climb up the trunk of a tree like a bear and not as would a chimpanzee or a gorilla, swinging up by the branches.

These first human beings (and their descendants) reached full maturity at twelve years of age and possessed a potential life span of about seventy-five years.

Many new emotions early appeared in these human twins. They experienced admiration for both objects and other beings and exhibited considerable vanity. But the most remarkable advance in emotional development was the sudden appearance of a new group of really human feelings, the worshipful group, embracing awe, reverence, humility, and even a primitive form of gratitude. Fear, joined with ignorance of natural phenomena, is about to give birth to primitive religion.

Not only were such human feelings manifested in these primitive humans, but many more highly evolved sentiments were also present in rudimentary form. They were mildly cognizant of

41

pity, shame, and reproach and were acutely conscious of love, hate, and revenge, being also susceptible to marked feelings of jealousy.

These first two humans — the twins — were a great trial to their Primates parents. They were so curious and adventurous that they nearly lost their lives on numerous occasions before they were eight years old. As it was, they were rather well scarred up by the time they were twelve." (Paper 62, Section 5, Para. 1-6)

The story of *Andon* and *Fonta, the first two human beings,* is a splendid account of the beginnings of the human race. The Revelators thought it important to share with us the story of their struggle. Perhaps in sharing their story, we would begin to grasp more fully, our origins as well as our destiny as a progressive race.

The Revelators write:

"After Andon and Fonta had decided to flee northward, they succumbed to their fears for a time, especially the fear of displeasing their father and immediate family. They envisaged being set upon by hostile relatives and thus recognized the possibility of meeting death at the hands of their already jealous tribesmen. As youngsters, the twins had spent most of their time in each other's company and for this reason had never been overly popular with their animal cousins of the Primates tribe. Nor had they improved their standing in the tribe by building a separate, and a very superior, tree home.

And it was in this new home among the treetops, one night after they had been awakened by a violent storm, and as they held each other in fearful and fond embrace, that they finally and fully made up their minds to flee from the tribal habitat and the home treetops." (Paper 63, Section 2, Para. 1, 2)

It is a beautifully detailed narrative of their courage to flee and begin a new life.

At the age of twelve, the twins Andon and Fonta agreed to depart from their pre-human parents, traveling northward from the hills of what is now Afghanistan to Europe. There, they would to make their own way in a savage world. The narrative tells of the tragedy of how their parents died fighting off savage gibbons as the two young siblings made haste their flight to the north. The observing celestial agents noted Andon and Fonta's first prayer for guidance, the first such supplication ever to occur on Earth, marking the first real worshipful attitude coming from a material being on our world.

North the two traveled, away from the less progressive cousins, to start their own family. In the end, Andon and Fonta fostered more than a dozen offspring, and almost fifty grandchildren. The parents died in the early their forties when rocks crushed them during a violent earthquake, but the progeny survived and became known as the *Andonic Race*, the first Aboriginal people.

The story of Andon and Fonta, Earth's ***first human family***, remains one of the most emotional moving narratives to be read anywhere. And there are many others stories of the development of man through the long ages spanning hundreds of thousands of years. The Revelators say the presentation of history was specifically done in order for man to gain a more complete understanding of his origins. If we knew where we came from, perhaps it would give us a much more enlightened view of where we are going.

The authors make it clear that evolution is not *an accident* and every phase of life is intelligently controlled and, prior to the appearance of creatures capable of *will*, spiritual forces manipulate environmental conditions so that intelligent life will result. It is also inferred that every evolutionary world is different in that depending on the geological and atmospheric conditions of each respective sphere, life forms develop differently and at a different pace. The Revelators state specifically that six hundred millions years ago, *Life Carrier Sons* (of a Divine Order) introduced a *sodium-chloride pattern of life* which could only be initiated once our oceans contained enough salt. Once this "briny mixture" was compatible and sustained, life was initiated, and thus, all life forms sprang from this original pattern.

Starting with a chronological overview of life's primordial beginnings on our world, including the successive steps of simple-celled life forms giving way to more complex organisms, the revelatory text tells the story earth's early history, like a modern day biology text, leaving no stone unturned on how marine, vegetable and eventually animal life was initiated some 600,000,000 years ago:

"The Life Carriers (Divine Sons who are charged with initiating life on evolutionary world) had projected a sodium chloride pattern of life; therefore no steps could be taken toward planting it until the ocean waters had become sufficiently briny. The Urantia type of protoplasm can function only in a suitable salt solution. All ancestral life — vegetable and animal — evolved in a salt-solution habitat. And even the more highly organized land animals could not continue to live did not this same essential salt solution circulate throughout their bodies in the blood stream which freely bathes, literally submerses, every tiny living cell in this "briny deep."

Your primitive ancestors freely circulated about in the salty ocean; today, this same ocean-like salty solution freely circulates about in your bodies, bathing each individual cell with a chemical liquid in all essentials comparable to the salt water which stimulated the first protoplasmic reactions of the first living cells to function on the planet. (Paper 58, Section 1, Para. 4, 5)

In describing the appearance of life, the following excerpt lays out the plan of intelligently guided evolution:

"The Evolutionary Panorama"

"The story of man's ascent from seaweed to the lordship of earthly creation is indeed a romance of biologic struggle and mind survival. Man's primordial ancestors were literally the slime and ooze of the ocean bed in the sluggish and warm-water bays and lagoons of the vast shore lines of the ancient inland seas, those very waters in which the Life Carriers established the three independent life implantations on Urantia.

Very few species of the early types of marine vegetation that participated in those epochal changes which resulted in the animal like borderland organisms are in existence today. The sponges are the survivors of one of these early midway types, those organisms through which the gradual transition from the vegetable to the animal took place. These early transition forms, while not identical with modern sponges, were much like them; they were true borderline organisms – neither vegetable nor animal – but they eventually led to the development of the true animal forms of life.

The bacteria, simple vegetable organisms of a very primitive nature, are very little changed from the early dawn of life; they even exhibit a degree of retrogression in their parasitic behavior. Many of the fungi also represent a retrograde movement in evolution, being plants which have lost their chlorophyll-making ability and have become more or less parasitic. The majority of disease-causing bacteria and their auxiliary virus bodies really belong to this group of renegade parasitic fungi. During the intervening ages the entire vast kingdom of plant life has evolved from ancestors from which the bacteria have also descended.

The higher protozoan type of animal life soon appeared, and appeared suddenly. And from these far-distant times the amoeba, the typical single-celled animal organism, has come on down but little modified. He disports himself today much as he did when he was the last and greatest achievement in life evolution. This minute creature and his protozoan cousins are to the animal creation what bacteria are to the plant kingdom; they represent the survival of the first early evolutionary steps in life differentiation together with failure of subsequent development.

Before long the early single-celled animal types associated themselves in communities, first on the plan of the Volvox and presently along the lines of the Hydra and jellyfish. Still later there evolved the starfish, stone lilies, sea urchins, sea cucumbers, centipedes, insects, spiders, crustaceans, and the closely related groups of earthworms and leeches, soon followed by the mollusks – the oyster, octopus, and snail. Hundreds upon hundreds of species intervened and perished; mention is made only of those which survived the long, long struggle. Such nonprogressive specimens, together with the later appearing fish family, today represent the stationary types of early and lower animals, branches of the tree of life which failed to progress.

The stage was thus set for the appearance of the first backboned animals, the fishes. From this fish family there sprang two unique modifications, the frog and the salamander. And it was the frog which began that series of progressive differentiations in animal life that finally culminated in man himself.

The frog is one of the earliest of surviving human-race ancestors, but it also failed to progress, persisting today much as in those remote times. The frog is the only species ancestor of the early dawn races now living on the face of the earth. The human race has no surviving ancestry between the frog and the Eskimo.

The frogs gave rise to the Reptilia, a great animal family which is virtually extinct, but which, before passing out of existence, gave origin to the whole bird family and the numerous orders of mammals.

Probably the greatest single leap of all prehuman evolution was executed when the reptile became a bird. The bird types of today – eagles, ducks, pigeons, and ostriches – all descended from the enormous reptiles of long, long ago.

The kingdom of reptiles, descended from the frog family, is today represented by four surviving divisions: two nonprogressive, snakes and lizards, together with their cousins, alligators and turtles; one partially progressive, the bird family, and the fourth, the ancestors of mammals and the direct line of descent of the human species. But though long departed the massiveness of the passing Reptilia found echo in the elephant and mastodon, while their peculiar forms were perpetuated in the leaping kangaroos.

Only fourteen phyla have appeared on Urantia, the fishes being the last, and no new classes have developed since birds and mammals.

It was from an agile little reptilian dinosaur of carnivorous habits but having a comparatively large brain that the placental mammals suddenly sprang. These mammals developed rapidly and in many different ways, not only giving rise to the common modern varieties but also evolving into marine types, such as whales and seals, and into air navigators like the bat family.

46

Man thus evolved from the higher mammals derived principally from the western implantation of life in the ancient east-west sheltered seas. The eastern and central groups of living organisms were early progressing favorably toward the attainment of prehuman levels of animal existence. But as the ages passed, the eastern focus of life emplacement failed to attain a satisfactory level of intelligent prehuman status, having suffered such repeated and irretrievable losses of its highest types of germ plasm that it was forever shorn of the power to rehabilitate human potentialities.

Since the quality of the mind capacity for development in this eastern group was so definitely inferior to that of the other two groups, the Life Carriers, with the consent of their superiors, so manipulated the environment as further to circumscribe these inferior prehuman strains of evolving life. To all outward appearances the elimination of these inferior groups of creatures was accidental, but in reality it was altogether purposeful.

Later in the evolutionary unfolding of intelligence, the lemur ancestors of the human species were far more advanced in North America than in other regions; and they were therefore led to migrate from the arena of western life implantation over the Bering land bridge and down the coast to southwestern Asia, where they continued to evolve and to benefit by the addition of certain strains of the central life group. Man thus evolved out of certain western and central life strains but in the central to near-eastern regions.

In this way the life that was planted on Urantia evolved until the ice age, when man himself first appeared and began his eventful planetary career. And this appearance of primitive man on earth during the ice age was not just an accident; it was by design. The rigors and climatic severity of the glacial era were in every way adapted to the purpose of fostering the production of a hardy type of human being with tremendous survival endowment" (Paper 65, Section 2)

After its publication in 1955, Sadler shared the material with experts in the fields of botany, archaeology, geography and astronomy, asking if there were inconsistencies found in the writings. Impressively, the return correspondence to Sadler was positive; the facts were correct so far as the experts could tell, and certain stated scenarios still unproven by science, but contained in the Revelation, were at least plausible. In other words, the overall science presented passed scientific and archeological muster. Items that could not be confirmed did not contradict scientific fact. While some scientists argued then that the science in the Urantia Book seemed "elemental," the overall presentation was (and still is) consistent with modern science.

Even the Revelators make the point that revealed knowledge cannot be "too far ahead" of the times in which any revelation is presented, and for the purpose of explaining our evolutionary plan, there is this statement:

"The universe of universes, including this small world called Urantia, is not being managed merely to meet our approval nor just to suit our convenience, much less to gratify our whims and satisfy our curiosity. The wise and all-powerful beings who are responsible for universe management undoubtedly know exactly what they are about; and so it becomes Life Carriers and behooves mortal minds to enlist in patient waiting and hearty co-operation with the rule of wisdom, the reign of power, and the march of progress." (Paper 65, Section 5, Para. 3)

The several chapters of narrative tell of early mans' appearance, his early struggles with nature, how his first religious impulses began from his fear of natural phenomena, his discovery of fire, tools and his transition from a hunter to a herder and where differing civilizations began to take root. Several hundred pages are dedicated to man's early customs and how we developed socially over the thousands of years of time. Interestingly, there are several papers dedicated to the differing colored races and how superior strains of each respective colored race overcame or absorbed the inferior ones:

"500,000 years ago the Badonan tribes of the northwestern highlands of India became involved in another great racial

struggle. For more than one hundred years this relentless warfare raged, and when the long fight was finished, only about one hundred families were left. But these survivors were the most intelligent and desirable of all the then living descendants of Andon and Fonta.

And now, among these highland Badonites there was a new and strange occurrence. A man and woman living in the northeastern part of the then inhabited highland region began suddenly to produce a family of unusually intelligent children. This was the Sangik family, the ancestors of all of the six colored races of Urantia.

These Sangik children, nineteen in number, were not only intelligent above their fellows, but their skins manifested a unique tendency to turn various colors upon exposure to sunlight. Among these nineteen children were five red, two orange, four yellow, two green, four blue, and two indigo. These colors became more pronounced as the children grew older, and when these youths later mated with their fellow tribesmen, all of their offspring tended toward the skin color of the Sangik parent." (Paper 64, Section 5, Para. 1, 2, 3)

The Revelation goes on to say how the races spread out from the Highlands of India:

"When the colored descendants of the Sangik family began to multiply, and as they sought opportunity for expansion into adjacent territory, the fifth glacier, the third of geologic count, was well advanced on its southern drift over Europe and Asia. These early colored races were extraordinarily tested by the rigors and hardships of the glacial age of their origin. This glacier was so extensive in Asia that for thousands of year's migration to eastern Asia was cut off. And not until the later retreat of the Mediterranean Sea, consequent upon the elevation of Arabia, was it possible for them to reach Africa.

Thus it was that for almost one hundred thousand years these Sangik peoples spread out around the foothills and mingled together more or less, notwithstanding the peculiar but natural antipathy which early manifested itself between the different races.

The red men early began to migrate to the northeast, on the heels of the retreating ice, passing around the highlands of India and occupying all of northeastern Asia. They were closely followed by the yellow tribes, who subsequently drove them out of Asia into North America.

When the relatively pure-line remnants of the red race forsook Asia, there were eleven tribes, and they numbered a little over seven thousand men, women, and children. These tribes were accompanied by three small groups of mixed ancestry, the largest of these being a combination of the orange and blue races. These three groups never fully fraternized with the red man and early journeyed southward to Mexico and Central America, where they were later joined by a small group of mixed yellows and reds. These peoples all intermarried and founded a new and amalgamated race, one which was much less warlike than the pure-line red men. Within five thousand years this amalgamated race broke up into three groups, establishing the civilizations respectively of Mexico, Central America, and South America. The South American offshoot did receive a faint touch of the blood of Adam.

To a certain extent the early red and yellow men mingled in Asia, and the offspring of this union journeyed on to the east and along the southern seacoast and, eventually, were driven by the rapidly increasing yellow race onto the peninsulas and near-by islands of the sea. They are the present-day brown men.

The yellow race has continued to occupy the central regions of eastern Asia. Of all the six colored races they have survived in greatest numbers. While the yellow men now and then engaged in racial war, they did not carry on such incessant and relentless wars of extermination as were waged by the red, green, and orange men. These three races virtually destroyed themselves before they were finally all but annihilated by their enemies of other races.

Since the fifth glacier did not extend so far south in Europe, the way was partially open for these Sangik peoples to migrate to the northwest; and upon the retreat of the ice the blue men, together with a few other small racial groups, migrated westward along the old trails of the Andon tribes. They invaded Europe in successive waves, occupying most of the continent.

In Europe they soon encountered the Neanderthal descendants of their early and common ancestor, Andon. These older European Neanderthalers had been driven south and east by the glacier and thus were in position quickly to encounter and absorb their invading cousins of the Sangik tribes.

In general and to start with, the Sangik tribes were more intelligent than, and in most ways far superior to, the deteriorated descendants of the early Andonic plainsmen; and the mingling of these Sangik tribes with the Neanderthal peoples led to the immediate improvement of the older race. It was this infusion of Sangik blood, more especially that of the blue man, which produced that marked improvement in the Neanderthal peoples exhibited by the successive waves of increasingly intelligent tribes that swept over Europe from the east.

During the following interglacial period this new Neanderthal race extended from England to India. The remnant of the blue race left in the old Persian peninsula later amalgamated with certain others, primarily the yellow; and the resultant blend, subsequently somewhat up stepped by the violet race of Adam, has persisted as the swarthy nomadic tribes of modern Arabs.

All efforts to identify the Sangik ancestry of modern peoples must take into account the later improvement of the racial strains by the subsequent admixture of Adamic blood.

The superior races sought the northern or temperate climes, while the orange, green, and indigo races successively gravitated to Africa over the newly elevated land bridge which separated the westward retreating Mediterranean from the Indian Ocean.

The last of the Sangik peoples to migrate from their center of race origin was the indigo man. About the time the green man was killing off the orange race in Egypt and greatly weakening himself in so doing, the great black exodus started south through Palestine along the coast; and later, when these physically strong indigo peoples overran Egypt, they wiped the green man out of existence by sheer force of numbers. These indigo races absorbed the remnants of the orange man and much of the stock of the green man, and certain of the indigo tribes were considerably improved by this racial amalgamation.

And so it appears that Egypt was first dominated by the orange man, then by the green, followed by the indigo (black) man, and still later by a mongrel race of indigo, blue, and modified green men. But long before Adam arrived, the blue men of Europe and the mixed races of Arabia had driven the indigo race out of Egypt and far south on the African continent.

As the Sangik migrations draw to a close, the green and orange races are gone, the red man holds North America, the yellow man eastern Asia, the blue man Europe, and the indigo race has gravitated to Africa. India harbors a blend of the secondary Sangik races, and the brown man, a blend of the red and yellow, holds the islands off the Asiatic coast. An amalgamated race of rather superior potential occupies the highlands of South America. The purer Andonites live in the extreme northern regions of Europe and in Iceland, Greenland, and northeastern North America.

During the periods of farthest glacial advance the westernmost of the Andon tribes came very near being driven into the sea. They lived for years on a narrow southern strip of the present island of England. And it was the tradition of these repeated glacial advances that drove them to take to the sea when the sixth and last glacier finally appeared. They were the first marine adventurers. They built boats and started in search of new lands which they hoped might be free from the terrifying ice invasions. And some of them reached Iceland, others Greenland, but the vast majority perished from hunger and thirst on the open sea.

A little more than eighty thousand years ago, shortly after the red man entered northwestern North America, the freezing over of the north seas and the advance of local ice fields on Greenland drove these Eskimo descendants of the Urantia aborigines to seek a better land, a new home; and they were successful, safely crossing the narrow straits which then separated Greenland from the northeastern land masses of North America. They reached the continent about twenty-one hundred years after the red man arrived in Alaska. Subsequently some of the mixed stock of the blue man journeyed westward and amalgamated with the later-day

Eskimos, and this union was slightly beneficial to the Eskimo tribes.

About five thousand years ago a chance meeting occurred between an Indian tribe and a lone Eskimo group on the southeastern shores of Hudson Bay. These two tribes found it difficult to communicate with each other, but very soon they intermarried with the result that these Eskimos were eventually absorbed by the more numerous red men. And this represents the only contact of the North American red man with any other human stock down to about one thousand years ago, when the white man first chanced to land on the Atlantic coast.

The struggles of these early ages were characterized by courage, bravery, and even heroism. And we all regret that so many of those sterling and rugged traits of your early ancestors have been lost to the later-day races. While we appreciate the value of many of the refinements of advancing civilization, we miss the magnificent persistency and superb devotion of your early ancestors, which oftentimes bordered on grandeur and sublimity."
(Paper 64)

Isn't it fascinating that this comprehensive detail of the colored races of earth has never been given serious attention by any modern scientific periodical?

And yet, if you were to Google "Origin of Colored Races," not until the Urantia Book is listed are there any single scientific or anthropological websites or articles dedicated to explaining why there are even differing races of color in the first place. Oddly, the last time there was any meaningful discussion, at least publicly, was in the early 19th Century when Darwin's 'Origin of Species,' was debated by others who claimed colored races only dates back to the sons of Noah, and that identifiably, only two races of colored existed, namely black and white.

The Urantia Book states the purpose for colored races, again, outlining a plan of intent and not random or arbitrary:

"There are many good and sufficient reasons for the plan of evolving either three or six colored races on the worlds of space.

Though Urantia mortals may not be in a position fully to appreciate all of these reasons, we would call attention to the following:

1. Variety is indispensable to opportunity for the wide functioning of natural selection, differential survival of superior strains.

2. Stronger and better races are to be had from the interbreeding of diverse peoples when these different races are carriers of superior inheritance factors. And the Urantia races would have benefited by such an early amalgamation provided such a conjoint people could have been subsequently effectively up-stepped by a thoroughgoing admixture with the superior Adamic stock.

3. Competition is healthfully stimulated by diversification of races.

4. Differences in status of the races and of groups within each race are essential to the development of human tolerance and altruism.

5. Homogeneity of the human race is not desirable until the peoples of an evolving world attain comparatively high levels of spiritual development." (Paper 64, Section 6, Para. 30-35)

Evolution is purposeful, not random. Life has purpose and direction, our universe is one large, vast training arena for mind, matter and spirit development. Are these things, so diligently narrated, not worthy of consideration or discussion? Is this not what all great religions and faiths tell us that life has meaning and is not some accident or undirected cause-and-effect reaction playing itself out blindly?

Unorthodox as it may seem, the Urantia Book does seem to specifically explain life in a seemingly logical manner.

And as we will see in the following chapter, even in heaven, life is purposeful, but it is not perfect.

6 THE EFFECTS OF THE LUCIFER REBELLION ON OUR CIVILIZATION

"When people began to multiply on the face of the ground, and daughters were born to them, the sons of God saw that they were fair; and they took wives for themselves of all that they chose. Then the LORD said, "My spirit shall not abide in mortals forever, for they are flesh; their days shall be one hundred twenty years."

"The Nephilim were on the earth in those days - and also afterward - when the sons of God went in to the daughters of humans, who bore children to them. These were the heroes that were of old, warriors of renown." (Genesis Chapter 6)

The Urantia Book states that about the time the six colored races began to disperse through Asia, Europe, Africa (and later into North America) some 500, 000 years ago, long before recorded history, a divine Son by the name of *Caligastia* arrived on our world with the *intent of teaching basic culture to the races of men.*

All evolutionary worlds, during the early stages of development are afforded a *Planetary Prince.* On our world, the arrival of the Planetary Prince and his staff represented the first *revelation* of truth to mankind.

This is the plan as it is carried out on all worlds of evolution, according to the Urantia Book:

"The Planetary Prince and his assistant brethren represent the nearest personalized approach (aside from incarnation) that the Eternal Son of Paradise can make to the creatures of time and space. True, the Creator Son touches the creatures of the realms through his spirit, but the Planetary Prince is the last of the orders of personal Sons extending out from Paradise to the children of men. The Infinite Spirit comes very near in the persons of the guardians of destiny and other angelic beings; the Universal Father lives in man by the prepersonal presence of (His spirit) the Mystery Monitors; but the Planetary Prince represents the last effort of the Eternal Son and his Sons to draw near you. On a newly inhabited world the Planetary Prince is the sole representative of complete divinity, springing from the Creator Son (the offspring of the Universal Father and the Eternal Son) and the Divine Minister (the universe Daughter of the Infinite Spirit).

The prince of a newly inhabited world is surrounded by a loyal corps of helpers and assistants and by large numbers of the ministering spirits. But the directing corps of such new worlds must be of the lower orders of the administrators of a system in order to be innately sympathetic with, and understanding of, the planetary problems and difficulties.
(Paper 50, Section 1)

For almost 300,000 thousand years Caligistia, his assistant *Daligastia* and a staff of one-hundred materialized *Jerusem* citizens (his corporeal staff, who would later become the founders of the *Nodite Tribe* or race of superior men and woman) were to setup a superior civilization in what is now the area between the Euphrates and the Tigris rivers in Iraq near the Persian Gulf. There, they taught the tribes of man agriculture, sanitary practices, communal living and tried to institute the basic tenets of basic trade practices. Early man was also taught basic math and was given to learning a basic alphabet (remembering that Cain, in the Old Testament traveled *"East to the Land of Nod"*).

In addition to teaching man basic skills of living together, an attempt was made to teach man basic spiritual principles, namely, the one-God concept. To these early races of men, the staff of Caligastia, wholly visible to the tribes of early man, seemed like gods themselves. This all was said to occur southern Iraq, the city of *Dalmatia*.

The laws of entrance to this city of Dalmatia were that those who entered the city had to adhere to the 'seven commandments' (which have been passed down through time and eventually became known as *The Ten Commandments*).

This is how the Urantia Book describes these ancient times as they unfolded on our earth almost half a million years ago:

"The headquarters of the Planetary Prince was situated in the Persian Gulf region of those days, in the district corresponding to later Mesopotamia.

The climate and landscape in the Mesopotamia of those times were in every way favorable to the undertakings of the Prince's staff and their assistants, very different from conditions which have sometimes since prevailed. It was necessary to have such a favoring climate as a part of the natural environment designed to induce primitive Urantians to make certain initial advances in culture and civilization. The one great task of those ages was to transform man from a hunter to a herder, with the hope that later on he would evolve into a peace-loving, home-abiding farmer.

The headquarters of the Planetary Prince on Urantia was typical of such stations on a young and developing sphere. The nucleus of the Prince's settlement was a very simple but beautiful city, enclosed within a wall forty feet high. This world center of culture was named Dalamatia in honor of Daligastia.

The city was laid out in ten subdivisions with the headquarters mansions of the ten councils of the corporeal staff situated at the centers of these subdivisions. Centermost in the city was the temple of the unseen Father. The administrative headquarters of the Prince and his associates was arranged in twelve chambers immediately grouped about the temple itself.

The buildings of Dalamatia were all one story except the council headquarters, which were two stories, and the central temple of the Father of all, which was small but three stories in height.

The city represented the best practices of those early days in building material — brick. Very little stone or wood was used. Home building and village architecture among the surrounding peoples were greatly improved by the Dalamatian example.

Near the Prince's headquarters there dwelt all colors and strata of human beings. And it was from these near-by tribes that the first students of the Prince's schools were recruited. Although these early schools of Dalamatia were crude, they provided all that could be done for the men and women of that primitive age.

The Prince's corporeal staff continuously gathered about them the superior individuals of the surrounding tribes and, after training and inspiring these students, sent them back as teachers and leaders of their respective peoples.

Early Days of the One Hundred

The arrival of the Prince's staff created a profound impression. While it required almost a thousand years for the news to spread abroad, those tribes near the Mesopotamian headquarters were tremendously influenced by the teachings and conduct of the one hundred new sojourners on Urantia. And much of your subsequent mythology grew out of the garbled legends of these early days when these members of the Prince's staff were repersonalized on Urantia as supermen." (Paper 66, Section 3 & 4)

At about the time Caligastia and the one-hundred assistants were creating the beginnings of what they had planned to be the cradle of a later appearing civilization, something went horribly wrong. The effect of what would transpire has had a long-lasting effect on humanity, and we have been paying a heavy price ever since. While much of what transpired then remains in very garbled form in our Biblical records, the fact of a universal rebellion, instigated by a high spiritual Son named *Lucifer*, did in fact take place, according to the authors of the Urantia Book:

"Lucifer was not an ascendant being; he was a created Son of the local universe, and of him it was said: "You were perfect in all your ways from the day you were created till unrighteousness was found in you." Many times had he been in counsel with the Most Highs of Edentia (the Capital sphere of our constellation of 100,000 worlds). And Lucifer reigned "upon the holy mountain of God," the administrative mount of Jerusem, for he was the chief executive of a great system of 607 inhabited worlds.

Lucifer was a magnificent being, a brilliant personality; he stood next to the Most High Fathers of the constellations in the direct line of universe authority. Notwithstanding Lucifer's transgression, subordinate intelligences refrained from showing him disrespect and disdain prior to Michael's bestowal on Urantia. Even the archangel of Michael, at the time of Moses' resurrection, "did not bring against him an accusing judgment but simply said, 'the Judge rebuke you.'" Judgment in such matters belongs to the Ancients of Days, the rulers of the superuniverse.

Lucifer is now the fallen and deposed Sovereign of Satania (the name of our local system). Self-contemplation is most disastrous, even to the exalted personalities of the celestial world. Of Lucifer it was said: "Your heart was lifted up because of your beauty; you corrupted your wisdom because of your brightness." Your olden prophet saw his sad estate when he wrote: "How are you fallen from heaven, O Lucifer, son of the morning! How are you cast down, you who dared to confuse the worlds!"

Very little was heard of Lucifer on Urantia owing to the fact that he assigned his first lieutenant, Satan, to advocate his cause on your planet. Satan was a member of the same primary group of Lanonandeks (a high order of Sons charged with the administration of system affairs) but had never functioned as a System Sovereign; he entered fully into the Lucifer insurrection. The "devil" is none other than Caligastia, the deposed Planetary Prince of Urantia and a Son of the secondary order of Lanonandeks. At the time Michael was on Urantia in the flesh (as Jesus), Lucifer, Satan, and Caligastia were leagued together to effect the miscarriage of his bestowal mission. But they signally failed.

Abaddon was the chief of the staff of Caligastia. He followed his master into rebellion and has ever since acted as chief executive of the Urantia rebels. Beelzebub was the leader of the disloyal midway creatures (Nephilim) who allied themselves with the forces of the traitorous Caligastia.

The dragon eventually became the symbolic representation of all these evil personages. Upon the triumph of Michael, "Gabriel came down and bound the dragon (all the rebel leaders) for an age." Of the Jerusem seraphic rebels it is written: "And the angels who kept not their first estate but left their own habitation, he has reserved in sure chains of darkness to the judgment of the great day." (Paper 56, Section 1)

And this represents a portion of the narrative giving account to an event the celestial authors' say took place 250,000 years ago in the "the heavens."

This story has survived in fragments on the pages of our bible. The "war in Heaven" so often talked about in Sunday school and on religious television is exhaustively re-told on the pages of the revelatory text:

Lucifer was a created personality of high esteem in the spiritual order. Under his administrative jurisdiction, Lucifer controlled a host of personalities who administered a system of worlds, both spiritual and evolutionary.

Over a period of time Lucifer began to challenge the truth of an unseen First Source and Center (God). This Son did not believe in an unseen force called God, and that the authority of the Supreme Rulers was falsely based on this ambiguous First Source and Center of all things.

Lucifer proclaimed in his manifesto that the Universal Father did not really exist, that physical gravity and space-energy were inherent in the universe, and that the Father was a myth invented by the Paradise Sons in order to enable them to maintain the rule of the universes in the Father's name. He denied that personality was a gift of the Universal Father. Lucifer maintained that far too much time and energy were expended upon the scheme of so thoroughly training ascending mortals in the principles of universe administration, principles which he alleged were unethical and unsound and further, he advocated that ascenders should enjoy **the liberty of individual self-determination**. He challenged and condemned the entire plan of mortal ascension as sponsored by the Paradise Sons of God and as supported by the Infinite Spirit.

"Self-assertion was the battle cry of the Lucifer rebellion. One of his chief arguments was that, if self-government was good and right for the Melchizedeks and other groups, it was equally good for all orders of intelligence. He was bold and persistent in the advocacy of the "equality of mind" and "the brotherhood of intelligence." He maintained that all government should be limited to the local planets and their voluntary confederation into the local systems. All other supervision he disallowed. He promised the Planetary Princes that they should rule the worlds as supreme executives. He denounced the location of legislative activities on the constellation headquarters and the conduct of judicial affairs on the universe capital. He contended that all these functions of government should be concentrated on the system capitals and proceeded to set up his own legislative assembly and organized his own tribunals under the jurisdiction of Satan. And he directed that the princes on the apostate worlds do the same." (Paper 53, Section 4)

These charges initiated a real rebellion, and although there were no physical wars between those who sided with Lucifer and those who sided with Michael, thousands of lower orders of Sons along with a significant percentage of angelic and seraphic orders began to embrace Lucifer's ideas of self-assertion and they joined him in challenging the authority of Michael, since his authority and rule was based on the supremacy of the unseen Father, a Father Lucifer asserted did not exist.

Note this paragraph found in the *New Testament*:

"And there was war in heaven. Michael and his angels fought against the dragon, and the dragon and his angels fought back. But he was not strong enough, and they lost their place in heaven. The great dragon was hurled down--that ancient serpent called the devil, or Satan, who leads the whole world astray. He was hurled to the earth, and his angels with him." - Revelations 12:7-9

From Paper 53, section 5 of the Urantia Book:

"There was war in heaven; Michael's commander and his angels fought against the dragon (Lucifer, Satan, and the apostate princes); and the dragon and his rebellious angels fought but prevailed not." This "war in heaven" was not a physical battle as such a conflict might be conceived on Urantia. In the early days of the struggle Lucifer held forth continuously in the planetary amphitheater. Gabriel conducted an unceasing exposure of the rebel sophistries from his headquarters taken up near at hand. The various personalities present on the sphere who were in doubt as to their attitude would journey back and forth between these discussions until they arrived at a final decision.

But this war in heaven was very terrible and very real. While displaying none of the barbarities so characteristic of physical warfare on the immature worlds, this conflict was far more deadly; material life is in jeopardy in material combat, but the war in heaven was fought in terms of life eternal"

The Revelators say this rebellion went on for seven years, in which time, Lucifer was able to run his own affairs as he saw fit. Many of whom who were fooled by the brilliance of Lucifer were given time to reconcile their position, or were later imprisoned (quarantined) with Lucifer, his assistant Satan and other orders of spirit personalities who 'fell' with him (embraced his doctrine of self-liberty and self-assertion).

In the end, Lucifer was stripped of his authority and placed in detention, where he awaits final adjudication by the *Ancients of Days*. Another High Son named Lanaforge has since replaced Lucifer and is now the spiritual "governor" of a system of 1,000 evolutionary worlds comprising a system of which our world is a part.

The Urantia Book says this event found its way on the pages of the Old and New Testament as it was handed down through man's early history. It appears as an event of legend, but in fact the "real war in heaven," was a war of ideology, one in which a spiritual personality of a high order proclaimed himself as supreme ruler and who believed that self-liberty and self-rule was the better method of spiritual administration throughout the grand universe.

Remembering, that at about the time of the Lucifer Rebellion our world was over the watch care of Caligastia, charged with the social uplifting of the then primitive population living on earth approximately 250,000 years ago. He was not visible, but his subordinates were. He cast his lost with Lucifer, and our world was thrown into chaos.

Caligastia embraced the self-assertion concepts, instructed his staff of seraphic helpers and materialized assistants to side with him and proclaimed himself 'God of Earth.' No longer did he abide by the principles as they are set forth on high, but chose instead to initiate their own methods for running the affairs of this world.

The whole purpose of spiritual and cultural revelation by Caligastia and his staff had been twisted; man's foundation for a progressively evolving society was in shambles, and what should have been the beginning of a long, increasingly settled and ever-perfecting world of varying races and cultures, disintegrated within fifty-years following the rebellion, left early evolving man without guidance and with only a vague memory of tiny morsels of truth.

Man, the Revelators say, suffered a serious blow. He fell back into his primitive state very quickly and remained so up until the arrival of Adam and Eve some 213,000 years later.

Only the work of Van, the leader of the loyal members of Caligastia's staff who refused to join the rebellion, journeyed northward and had any hope of making a long-term difference in the social development of mankind. Van now has a lake in northeastern Turkey named in his honor. *Lake Van* was, far back in man's early and forgotten history, the settlement of an ancient culture (The *Urartians* among them), which, over time found its way interwoven into the legends of early man.

Some remnants of a superior culture and thousands of folklore describing this long-ago culture are found today throughout this region.

Man did not have the revelatory guidance that is normally afforded normal evolutionary worlds. The celestial authors say much of our modern dilemma stems from the lack of true spiritual foundation that should have been planted with the help from these long ago brilliant sons who went astray because they were deceived during the Lucifer Rebellion. But they also caution us that despite the traitorous Caligastia, man is still held in safety by the Father's spirit:

"The doctrine of a personal devil on Urantia, though it had some foundation in the planetary presence of the traitorous and iniquitous Caligastia, was nevertheless wholly fictitious in its teachings that such a "devil" could influence the normal human mind against its free and natural choosing. Even before Michael's bestowal on Urantia (as Jesus), neither Caligastia nor Daligastia was ever able to oppress mortals or to coerce any normal individual into doing anything against the human will. The free will of man is supreme in moral affairs; even the indwelling spirit of God refuses to compel man to think a single thought or to perform a single act against the choosing of man's own will." (Paper 66, Section 8)

The immediate, as well as long-term effects of this heavenly rebellion, is that it left our embryonic civilization with little foundation from which to grow. Early man was left isolated, spiritual truth was distorted and for the most part absent, and the basic tenets of civilization were never afforded a real opportunity to flourish.

For the next two hundred thousand years, man had to go it alone, except for the few members of Caligastia's staff, namely Van and his human associate Amadon, who remained loyal to the

Fathers' universal plan, and these faithful Son's did try to forge ahead and build an enduring civilization in eastern Turkey.

As to the present status of his long ago rebellion:

"The rebellion has ended on Jerusem. It ends on the fallen worlds as fast as divine Sons arrive (just as it was settled when Jesus, the Creator Son confronted Lucifer and Satan and issued the now famous proclamation of "get you behind me Satan"). *We believe that all rebels who will ever accept mercy have done so. We await the flashing broadcast that will deprive these traitors of personality existence. We anticipate the verdict of Uversa will be announced by the executionary broadcast which will effect the annihilation of these interned rebels. Then will you look for their places, but they shall not be found.* "And they who know you among the worlds will be astonished at you; you have been a terror, but never shall you be any more." *And thus shall all of these unworthy traitors* "become as though they had not been." *All await the Uversa decree."* (Paper 53, Section 9)

Our ancient historical records seem to corroborate a tradition of just such a rebellion occurring. Many view the story as myth, but like all myths, where do they find origin? Names like *Abaddon, Beelzebub, Satan* and other names do appear littered in ancient writings, including many names who appear in our own Bible. Is it possible the Urantia Book account is not so incredulous? It does seem to tie a lot of loose ends together.

But to a greater point, the Urantia Book narrative discloses that there is a real civilization "in heaven;" that real personalities do exist and real events such as The Lucifer Rebellion can and do take place from time to time, events which show that heaven, while not perfect, is still vibrant, active and just as busy as life here on our little world spinning in space.

7 THE REAL STORY OF ADAM AND EVE

Authors' note: Prior to reading this chapter I would encourage the reader to review the online Wikipedia descriptions of the various beliefs pertaining to the origins of Adam and Eve. In doing so one will have a fuller appreciation of just how influential these two personalities have become with regard to our early religious and cultural tradition. It will also provide insight as to the Urantia Book narrative I will now summarize:

"And the LORD God formed man of the dust of the ground, and breathed into his nostrils the breath of life; and man became a living soul.
And the LORD God planted a garden eastward in Eden; and there he put the man whom he had formed."
- Genesis 2: 7,8

Modern man views the story of Adam and Eve from several different perspectives. If you are a devout Christian and hold true the scriptural account, then Adam and Eve were the first humans to appear and were created in God's image. You also believe the Garden of Eden was a real place. It is the story of the ages. We were taught that Eve eating from the Tree of Knowledge was the first sin and was the cause of the consequent 'fall from grace' that led to the eviction of Adam and Eve from the Garden because of Eve 'eating the forbidden fruit.'

This story is richly embedded in our Judeo-Christian history which has survived for ages all around the world. It is *the* story of all stories and the metaphors have been an infinite source of Sunday school teachings.

But how much of the story is real, and from where does it find its origin?

The Urantia Book states that Adam and Eve were divine beings, they were a *revelation of truth* in that they were spiritual in origin and *divine in heritage*. They came here to improve the spiritual as well as biological well-being of our races.

Even though the common belief is that Adam and Eve were the first humans created by God, a careful examination of the story found in Genesis indicates that Adam and Eve were not the only humans in existence when they arrived or when they were 'created.'

Regarding Cain, following his slaying of Abel:

"Behold, thou hast driven me out this day from the face of the earth; and from thy face shall I be hid; and I shall be a fugitive and a vagabond in the earth; and it shall come to pass, that every one that findeth me shall slay me."

"And Cain went out from the presence of the LORD, and dwelt in the land of Nod, on the east of Eden."
    - Genesis 4: 14-16

And we know that it was here that Cain 'found himself a "wife.'

"Cain knew his wife, and she conceived and bore Enoch; and he built a city, and named it Enoch after his son Enoch." *- Genesis 4:17*

Here is how the Urantia Book describes the appearance of Adam and Eve on the day they arrived in the Garden, which had been prepared for them:

"Adam and Eve fell asleep on Jerusem (our system headquarters where they lived prior to coming here), and when they awakened in the Father's temple on Urantia in the presence of the mighty throng assembled to welcome them, they were face to face with two beings of whom they had heard much, Van and his faithful associate Amadon. These two heroes of the Caligastia secession were the first to welcome them in their new garden home.

The tongue of Eden was an Andonic dialect as spoken by Amadon. Van and Amadon had markedly improved this language by creating a new alphabet of twenty-four letters, and they had hoped to see it become the tongue of Urantia as the Edenic culture would spread throughout the world. Adam and Eve had fully mastered this human dialect before they departed from Jerusem so that this son of Andon heard the exalted ruler of his world address him in his own tongue.

And on that day there was great excitement and joy throughout Eden as the runners went in great haste to the rendezvous of the carrier pigeons assembled from near and far, shouting: "Let loose the birds; let them carry the word that the promised Son has come." Hundreds of believer settlements had faithfully, year after year, kept up the supply of these home-reared pigeons for just such an occasion.

As the news of Adam's arrival spread abroad, thousands of the near-by tribesmen accepted the teachings of Van and Amadon, while for months and month's pilgrims continued to pour into Eden to welcome Adam and Eve and to do homage to their unseen Father." (Paper 74, Section 2)

Consider the following account pertaining to Adam inspecting the Garden and how this account has been converted into the Biblical story of God creating the world in six days:

"The story of the creation of Urantia in six days was based on the tradition that Adam and Eve had spent just six days in their initial survey of the Garden. This circumstance lent almost sacred sanction to the time period of the week, which had been originally

introduced by the Dalamatians. Adam's spending six days inspecting the Garden and formulating preliminary plans for organization was not prearranged; it was worked out from day to day. The choosing of the seventh day for worship was wholly incidental to the facts herewith narrated.

The legend of the making of the world in six days was an afterthought, in fact, more than thirty thousand years afterwards. One feature of the narrative, the sudden appearance of the sun and moon, may have taken origin in the traditions of the onetime sudden emergence of the world from a dense space cloud of minute matter which had long obscured both sun and moon.

The story of creating Eve out of Adam's rib is a confused condensation of the Adamic arrival and the celestial surgery connected with the interchange of living substances associated with the coming of the corporeal staff of the Planetary Prince more than four hundred and fifty thousand years previously.

The majority of the world's peoples have been influenced by the tradition that Adam and Eve had physical forms created for them upon their arrival on Urantia. The belief in man having been created from clay was well-nigh universal in the Eastern Hemisphere; this tradition can be traced from the Philippine Islands around the world to Africa. And many groups accepted this story of man's clay origin by some form of special creation in the place of the earlier beliefs in progressive creation — evolution." (Paper 74, Section 8)

The author's explain how we arrived at the current belief of Adam and Eve being the first two human beings, and further, how this legend became accepted into our religious heritage over time:

"The Babylonians, because of immediate contact with the remnants of the civilization of the Adamites, enlarged and embellished the story of man's creation; they taught that he had descended directly from the gods. They held to an aristocratic origin for the race which was incompatible with even the doctrine of creation out of clay.

The Old Testament account of creation dates from long after the time of Moses; he never taught the Hebrews such a distorted story. But he did present a simple and condensed narrative of creation to the Israelites, hoping thereby to augment his appeal to worship the Creator, the Universal Father, whom he called the Lord God of Israel.

In his early teachings, Moses very wisely did not attempt to go back of Adam's time, and since Moses was the supreme teacher of the Hebrews, the stories of Adam became intimately associated with those of creation. That the earlier traditions recognized pre-Adamic civilization is clearly shown by the fact that later editors, intending to eradicate all reference to human affairs before Adam's time, neglected to remove the telltale reference to Cain's emigration to the "land of Nod," where he took himself a wife.

The Hebrews had no written language in general usage for a long time after they reached Palestine. They learned the use of an alphabet from the neighboring Philistines, who were political refugees from the higher civilization of Crete. The Hebrews did little writing until about 900 B.C., and having no written language until such a late date, they had several different stories of creation in circulation, but after the Babylonian captivity they inclined more toward accepting a modified Mesopotamian version.

Jewish tradition became crystallized about Moses, and because he endeavored to trace the lineage of Abraham back to Adam, the Jews assumed that Adam was the first of all mankind. Yahweh was the creator, and since Adam was supposed to be the first man, he must have made the world just prior to making Adam. And then the tradition of Adam's six days got woven into the story, with the result that almost a thousand years after Moses' sojourn on earth the tradition of creation in six days was written out and subsequently credited to him.

When the Jewish priests returned to Jerusalem, they had already completed the writing of their narrative of the beginning of things. Soon they made claims that this recital was a recently discovered story of creation written by Moses. But the contemporary Hebrews of around 500 B.C. did not consider these writings to be divine revelations; they looked upon them much as later peoples regard mythological narratives.

This spurious document, reputed to be the teachings of Moses, was brought to the attention of Ptolemy, the Greek king of Egypt, who had it translated into Greek by a commission of seventy scholars for his new library at Alexandria. And so this account found its place among those writings which subsequently became a part of the later collections of the "sacred scriptures" of the Hebrew and Christian religions. And through identification with these theological systems, such concepts for a long time profoundly influenced the philosophy of many Occidental peoples.

The Christian teachers perpetuated the belief in the fiat creation of the human race, and all this led directly to the formation of the hypothesis of a onetime golden age of utopian bliss and the theory of the fall of man or superman which accounted for the nonutopian condition of society. These outlooks on life and man's place in the universe were at best discouraging since they were predicated upon a belief in retrogression rather than progression, as well as implying a vengeful Deity, who had vented wrath upon the human race in retribution for the errors of certain onetime planetary administrators.

The "golden age" is a myth, but Eden was a fact, and the Garden civilization was actually overthrown. Adam and Eve carried on in the Garden for one hundred and seventeen years when, through the impatience of Eve and the errors of judgment of Adam, they presumed to turn aside from the ordained way, speedily bringing disaster upon themselves and ruinous retardation upon the developmental progression of all Urantia." (Paper 74, Section 8)

The early descendants of Adam instituted model civilizations and cultures as they traveled around the world. Down through time, however, these higher cultures diminished as the still-primitive races that overran the earth absorbed them. The Revelation clearly states that at one time a superior race did exist:

Consider the following brief passage concerning Adams descendants:

"Adam left a great intellectual and spiritual culture behind him, but it was not advanced in mechanical appliances since every civilization is limited by available natural resources, inherent genius, and sufficient leisure to insure inventive fruition. The civilization of the violet race was predicated on the presence of Adam and on the traditions of the first Eden. After Adam's death and as these traditions grew dim through the passing millenniums, the cultural level of the Adamites steadily deteriorated until it reached a state of reciprocal balance with the status of the surrounding peoples and the naturally evolving cultural capacities of the violet race."

"But the Adamites were a real nation around 19,000 B.C., numbering four and a half million, and already they had poured forth millions of their progeny into the surrounding peoples."

While modern theology looks at Adams' fall from grace as the origin of sin the world, the Revelators painstakingly show that despite the failure of the Garden plan, which I will shortly summarize, man has benefited from their contribution, albeit not as much as what could have happened had Adam and Eve succeeded with the divine plan.

Adam and Eve lived on earth around 37,000 B.C. They are called *Material Sons;* Material Sons and Daughters are physical but their origins, unlike ascendant mortals of material worlds, are divine – they are created and they are the representatives of the Creator Son (Michael) *in material form*; they are exquisite and brilliant beings who serve various functions in the universe, from teachers on worlds of the resurrection to scientists and researchers on the heavenly capital spheres. In a sense, Material Sons and Daughters, Adam and Eve might be consider 'ambassadors' of the spiritual world:

"Material Sons vary in height from eight to ten feet, and their bodies glow with the brilliance of radiant light of a violet hue. While material blood circulates through their material bodies, they are also surcharged with divine energy and saturated with celestial light. These Material Sons (the Adams) and Material

Daughters (the Eves) are equal to each other, differing only in reproductive nature and in certain chemical endowments. They are equal but differential, male and female—hence complemental—and are designed to serve on almost all assignments in pairs." (Paper 51, Section 1, Para. 3)

The Urantia Book goes on to say all worlds of evolution receive an Adam and Eve when man reaches his *peak of evolutionary development*:

"When the original impetus of evolutionary life has run its biologic course, when man has reached the apex of animal development, there arrives the second order of sonship, and the second dispensation of grace and ministry is inaugurated. This is true on all evolutionary worlds. When the highest possible level of evolutionary life has been attained, when primitive man has ascended as far as possible in the biologic scale, a Material Son and Daughter always appear on the planet." (Paper 52, Section 3, Para. 1)

When Adam and Eve arrived on our world, our ancestors had reached his apex of biological development.

Remembering also, this was some 230,000 years *after* the Caligastia enterprise had fallen to pieces due to the Lucifer Rebellion and the subsequent misfortunes of Caligastia, whose initial plan of developing human culture had been disrupted during the years following the rebellion:

"Adam and Eve found themselves on a sphere wholly unprepared for the proclamation of the brotherhood of man, a world groping about in abject spiritual darkness and cursed with confusion worse confounded by the miscarriage of the mission of the preceding administration. Mind and morals were at a low level, and instead of beginning the task of effecting religious unity, they must begin all anew the work of converting the inhabitants to the simplest forms of religious belief. Instead of finding one language ready for adoption, they were confronted by the world-wide confusion of hundreds upon hundreds of local dialects. No

Adam of the planetary service was ever set down on a more difficult world; the obstacles seemed insuperable and the problems beyond creature solution.

They were isolated, and the tremendous sense of loneliness which bore down upon them was all the more heightened by the early departure of the Melchizedek receivers. Only indirectly, by means of the angelic orders, could they communicate with any being off the planet. Slowly their courage weakened, their spirits drooped, and sometimes their faith almost faltered.

And this is the true picture of the consternation of these two noble souls as they pondered the tasks which confronted them. They were both keenly aware of the enormous undertaking involved in the execution of their planetary assignment.

Probably no Material Sons of Nebadon were ever faced with such a difficult and seemingly hopeless task as confronted Adam and Eve in the sorry plight of Urantia. But they would have sometime met with success had they been more farseeing and patient. Both of them, especially Eve, were altogether too impatient; they were not willing to settle down to the long, long endurance test. They wanted to see some immediate results, and they did, but the results thus secured proved most disastrous both to themselves and to their world." (Paper 75, Section 1)

The Revelation details how this seemingly progressive plan of the Garden ended in tragedy just 117 years after Adam and Eve arrived on Earth.

What happened was this: Eve believed that much quicker progress could be made if she and a member of neighboring and superior Nodites (offspring of the original one-hundred materialized members of Caligastia's staff) could procreate a child, that this child would build a bond of trust between the Garden members and those of the surrounding Nodite Tribe.

"The fateful meeting occurred during the twilight hours of the autumn evening, not far from the home of Adam. Eve had never before met the beautiful and enthusiastic Cano — and he was a magnificent specimen of the survival of the superior physique and

outstanding intellect of his remote progenitors of the Prince's staff..."

"...Influenced by flattery, enthusiasm, and great personal persuasion, Eve then and there consented to embark upon the much-discussed enterprise, to add her own little scheme of world saving to the larger and more far-reaching divine plan. Before she quite realized what was transpiring, the fatal step had been taken. It was done." (Paper 75, Section 3)

And so Cain was born. Cano was the father and a member of the Nodites, a more advanced race of that region more receptive to the teachings of Adam and Eve. The narrative explains how Eve violated the divine plan, for Material beings of divine origin are forbidden to directly *procreate* with material beings of the world:

"Eve had consented to participate in the practice of good and evil (by mating with Cano). Good is the carrying out of the divine plans; sin is a deliberate transgression of the divine will; evil is the misadaptation of plans and the maladjustment of techniques resulting in universe disharmony and planetary confusion." (Paper 75, Section 4)

"Eve's disillusionment was truly pathetic. Adam discerned the whole predicament and, while heartbroken and dejected, entertained only pity and sympathy for his erring mate.

It was in the despair of the realization of failure that Adam, the day after Eve's misstep, sought out Laotta, the brilliant Nodite woman who was head of the western schools of the Garden, and with premeditation committed the folly of Eve. But do not misunderstand; Adam was not beguiled; he knew exactly what he was about; he deliberately chose to share the fate of Eve. He loved his mate with a super mortal affection, and the thought of the possibility of a lonely vigil on Urantia without her was more than he could endure."

"When they learned what had happened to Eve, the infuriated inhabitants of the Garden became unmanageable; they declared war on the near-by Nodite settlement. They swept out through the gates of Eden and down upon these unprepared people, utterly destroying them — not a man, woman, or child was spared. And Cano, the father of Cain yet unborn, also perished."
(Paper 75, Section 5)

The immediate ramifications of this act resulted in both Adam and Eve being stripped of their immortal status. Adam and Eve were left without aid of spiritual advisors from that point on and were told to do the best they could, but as mortals of the realm.

The secondary effect of this sexual liaison between a divine being and a mortal man resulted in warfare that broke out between the residents of the Garden and the Nodite Race. Within a short matter of time savages overran the Garden. Adam and Eve, their children and longtime-residents of the Eden were driven out, forced to relocate to a safer region.

Adam led his family eastward to what is now Iraq and it is here the remnants of this one-time race would ultimately build their civilization.

It is also stated that Eve's temptation of circumventing the divine plan was influenced by Caligastia, who had initiated the idea and persuaded Cano's father, Serapatatia, the superior leader of the Nodite tribe, to embrace the plan of bringing Eve and Cano together:

"Caligastia paid frequent visits to the Garden and held many conferences with Adam and Eve, but they were adamant to all his suggestions of compromise and short-cut adventures. They had before them enough of the results of rebellion to produce effective immunity against all such insinuating proposals. Even the young offspring of Adam were uninfluenced by the overtures of Daligastia. And of course neither Caligastia nor his associate had power to influence any individual against his will, much less to persuade the children of Adam to do wrong.

It must be remembered that Caligastia was still the titular Planetary Prince of Urantia, a misguided but nevertheless high Son of the local universe. He was not finally deposed until the times of Christ Michael on Urantia.

But the fallen Prince was persistent and determined. He soon gave up working on Adam and decided to try a wily flank attack on Eve. The evil one concluded that the only hope for success lay in the adroit employment of suitable persons belonging to the upper strata of the Nodite group, the descendants of his onetime corporeal-staff associates. And the plans were accordingly laid for entrapping the mother of the violet race." (Paper 75, Section 2)

"It should again be emphasized that Serapatatia was altogether honest and wholly sincere in all that he proposed. He never once suspected that he was playing into the hands of Caligastia and Daligastia. Serapatatia was entirely loyal to the plan of building up a strong reserve of the violet race before attempting the world-wide up stepping of the confused peoples of Urantia. But this would require hundreds of years to consummate, and he was impatient; he wanted to see some immediate results — something in his own lifetime. He made it clear to Eve that Adam was oftentimes discouraged by the little that had been accomplished toward uplifting the world." (Paper 75, Section 3)

But in the end, the plan was disastrous and Caligastia was able once again to thwart the spiritual and cultural affairs of man by appealing to the short-sighted, though sincere nature, of man's desires to take shortcuts:

"Never, in your entire ascent to Paradise, will you gain anything by impatiently attempting to circumvent the established and divine plan by short cuts, personal inventions, or other devices for improving on the way of perfection, to perfection, and for eternal perfection." (Paper 75, Section 8)

And it has been this episode of impatience that has scarred man's long history.

The Revelators say that had Adam and Eve not succumbed to trying to find immediate progress, and had they stayed the course, then the human race would have made much better progress than it did. If Adam and Eve had stayed the normal course, then the influence of these two divine beings might very well be present even today alongside a superior culture which would have been existence for over thirty-thousand years – as this is the *normal course* of a normal evolutionary world, according the authors of the Urantia Book.

As it stands, there are still conflicts in the Middle East (and throughout the world), warfare on our world is still prevalent, and spiritually speaking, we still view God from the perspective of men and women of prehistoric times.

Do the authors say mans' current state is the fault of Adam and Eve?

Not completely.

What it stated is that because of a lack of divine guidance, man has crawled his way, much to his own credit, to his current state *without* the enduring divine influence which would have helped us along the way:

"Adam and Eve did fall from their high estate of material sonship down to the lowly status of mortal man. But that was not the fall of man. The human race has been uplifted despite the immediate consequences of the Adamic default. Although the divine plan of giving the violet race to the Urantia peoples miscarried, the mortal races have profited enormously from the limited contribution which Adam and his descendants made to the Urantia races.

There has been no "fall of man." The history of the human race is one of progressive evolution, and the Adamic bestowal left the world peoples greatly improved over their previous biologic condition. The more superior stocks of Urantia now contain inheritance factors derived from as many as four separate sources: Andonite, Sangik, Nodite, and Adamic.

Adam should not be regarded as the cause of a curse on the human race. While he did fail in carrying forward the divine plan, while he did transgress his covenant with Deity, while he and his mate were most certainly degraded in creature status, notwithstanding all this, their contribution to the human race did much to advance civilization on Urantia. (Paper 75, Section 8)

Adam and Eve are part of a larger reality that encompasses the idea of man ascending upward and of God and his spirit family reaching out to help man in his ascent.

Of Adam and Eve's miscarriage of the divine plan to assist the human race:

"But it is not surprising that these missteps occur in the affairs of the evolutionary universes. We are a part of a gigantic creation, and it is not strange that everything does not work in perfection; our universe was not created in perfection. Perfection is our eternal goal, not our origin."

But in our evolving universe of relative perfection and imperfection we rejoice that disagreement and misunderstanding are possible, for thereby is evidenced the fact and the act of personality in the universe. And if our creation is an existence dominated by personality, then can you be assured of the possibilities of personality survival, advancement, and achievement; we can be confident of personality growth, experience, and adventure.

What a glorious universe, in that it is personal and progressive, not merely mechanical or even passively perfect!"
(Paper 75, Section 8)

Adam lived to the ripe old age of 530, Eve just 19 years shy of her mate. They built up a onetime great civilization in the Euphrates Valley, and for thousands of years, did the best they could to promote cultural advancement. Their children and grandchildren spread the seed of the violet race and mankind did benefit. Our sense of artistic expression, our sciences, our spiritual development, basic forms of government and our societal infrastructure all improved because of the Adamic race.

The Revelators portray the heroic efforts made by these long-forgotten men and women who brought at least some spiritual and cultural guidance to our ancestors. That Adam and Eve fell short of their mission of uplifting the human race in accordance with the divine plan does not in the least detract from the importance of what they did accomplish, and of some of the benefits we garnered as a result of their heroic – *if not misguided* - efforts.

8 THE MELCHIZEDEK MISSION

Having thus far explored the two previous revelations of truth, as explained in the Urantia Book, namely the truths presented first through the *Caligastia Plan,* and through the later appearance of *Adam and Eve* (divine personalities sent to our world *specifically* to introduce new concepts of spiritual truth to mankind), we now turn our attention to a particular order of *Sons* known as *Melchizedeks*, for these Sons are of a high order, and, according to the Urantia Book, have been influential in our early religious history.

"The Lord hath sworn, and will not repent, Thou art a priest for ever after the order of Melchizedek" - Psalms 110:4

"And Melchizedek king of Salem brought forth bread and wine: and he was the priest of the most high God." – Genesis 14:18

"For this Melchizedek, king of Salem, priest of the most high God, who met Abraham returning from the slaughter of the kings, and blessed him to whom also Abraham gave a tenth part of all; first being by interpretation King of righteousness, and after that also King of Salem, which is, King of peace; without father, without mother, without descent, having neither beginning of days, nor end of life; but made like unto the Son of God; abideth a priest continually." – Hebrews 7:1-3

The Urantia Book explains that Melchizedek came to our world in 1,973 B.C. because the one-God concept had all but faded from the minds of men during this age. Man had developed multiple deities, he worshiped and deified everything from rocks to animals, fire, volcanoes, weather phenomena, even the sun, the moon and the stars (which has evolved into astrology). Something had to be done to prepare man for the pending bestowal of Michael (Jesus), who would herald a new revelation of God the Father, but:

"Revealed truth was threatened with extinction during the millenniums which followed the miscarriage of the Adamic mission on Urantia. Though making progress intellectually, the human races were slowly losing ground spiritually. About 3000 B.C. the concept of God had grown very hazy in the minds of men." (Paper 93, Section 1, Para. 1)

"It was 1,973 years before the birth of Jesus that Machiventa was bestowed upon the human races of Urantia. His coming was unspectacular; his materialization was not witnessed by human eyes. He was first observed by mortal man on that eventful day when he entered the tent of Amdon, a Chaldean herder of Sumerian extraction. And the proclamation of his mission was embodied in the simple statement which he made to this shepherd, " I am Melchizedek, priest of El Elyon, the Most High, the one and only God. "

When the herder had recovered from his astonishment, and after he had plied this stranger with many questions, he asked Melchizedek to sup with him, and this was the first time in his long universe career that Machiventa had partaken of material food, the nourishment which was to sustain him throughout his ninety-four years of life as a material being.

And that night, as they talked out under the stars, Melchizedek began his mission of the revelation of the truth of the reality of God when, with a sweep of his arm, he turned to Amdon, saying, "El Elyon, the Most High, is the divine creator of the stars of the firmament and even of this very earth on which we live, and he is also the supreme God of heaven."

"Within a few years Melchizedek had gathered around himself a group of pupils, disciples, and believers who formed the nucleus of the later community of Salem. He was soon known throughout Palestine as the priest of El Elyon, the Most High, and as the sage of Salem. Among some of the surrounding tribes he was often referred to as the sheik, or king, of Salem. Salem was the site which after the disappearance of Melchizedek became the city of Jebus, subsequently being called Jerusalem.

With the passing of a decade, Melchizedek organized his schools at Salem, patterning them on the olden system which had been developed by the early Sethite priests of the second Eden. Even the idea of a tithing system, which was introduced by his later convert Abraham, was also derived from the lingering traditions of the methods of the ancient Sethites.

"...Melchizedek taught the concept of one God, a universal Deity" (Paper 99, Section 3, Para. 1-4)

"Like Jesus, Melchizedek attended strictly to the fulfillment of his mission of his bestowal. He did not attempt to reform the mores, to change the habits of the world, nor to promulgate even advanced sanitary practices or scientific truths. He came to achieve two tasks: to keep alive on earth the truth of the one God and to prepare the way for the subsequent mortal bestowal of a Paradise Son of that Universal Father." (Paper 93, Section 4, Para. 15)

"The teaching of Melchizedek was full and replete, but the records of these days seemed impossible and fantastic to the later Hebrew priests, although many had some understanding of these transactions, at least up to the times of the en masse editing of the Old Testament records in Babylon.

"What the Old Testament records describe as conversations between Abraham and God were in reality conferences between Abraham and Melchizedek. Later scribes regarded the term

Melchizedek as synonymous with God. The record of so many contacts of Abraham and Sarah with "the angel of the Lord" refers to their numerous visits with Melchizedek.

"The Hebrew narratives of Isaac, Jacob, and Joseph are far more reliable than those about Abraham, although they also contain many diversions from the facts, alterations made intentionally and unintentionally at the time of the compilation of these records by the Hebrew priests during the Babylonian captivity. Keturah was not a wife of Abraham; like Hagar, she was merely a concubine. All of Abraham's property went to Isaac, the son of Sarah, the status wife. Abraham was not so old as the records indicate, and his wife was much younger. These ages were deliberately altered in order to provide for the subsequent alleged miraculous birth of Isaac." (Paper 93, Section 8)

So what exactly is a Melchizedek Son?

Melchizedek Sons are the spiritual *offspring* of the Creator Son and the Daughter of the Infinite Spirit; they are a self-governing group of divine Sons who are of great assistance to the affairs of a local universe. The authors, in describing the nature and function of this divine order of beings, would be considered "the elder brothers" of the vast personalities who inhabit the universe:

"The Melchizedeks are the first order of divine Sons to approach sufficiently near the lower creature life to be able to function directly in the ministry of mortal uplift, to serve the evolutionary races without the necessity of incarnation. These Sons are naturally at the mid-point of the great personality descent, by origin being just about midway between the highest Divinity and the lowest creature life of will endowment. They thus become the natural intermediaries between the higher and divine levels of living existence and the lower, even the material, forms of life on the evolutionary worlds. The seraphic orders, the angels, delight to work with the Melchizedeks; in fact, all forms of intelligent life find in these Sons understanding friends, sympathetic teachers, and wise counselors.

The Melchizedeks are a self-governing order. With this unique group we encounter the first attempt at self-determination on the part of local universe beings and observe the highest type of true self-government.."

"...And it should be recorded that they have never abused their prerogatives; not once throughout all the superuniverse of Orvonton have these Melchizedek Sons ever betrayed their trust. They are the hope of every universe group which aspires to self-government; they are the pattern and the teachers of self-government to all the spheres of Nebadon. All orders of intelligent beings, superiors from above and subordinates from below, are wholehearted in their praise of the government of the Melchizedeks." *(Paper 35, Section 2, Para. 1, 2)*

It is the mission of these Sons to go out to the various worlds and assist in the general running of administrative affairs on behalf of Michael and in representative of Gabriel:

"The Melchizedeks function as mobile and advisory review courts of the realms; these universe Sons go in small groups to the worlds to serve as advisory commissions, to take depositions, to receive suggestions, and to act as counselors, thus helping to compose the major difficulties and settle the serious differences which arise from time to time in the affairs of the evolutionary domains.

"These eldest Sons of a universe are the chief aids of the Bright and Morning Star in carrying out the mandates of the Creator Son. When a Melchizedek goes to a remote world in the name of Gabriel, he may, for the purposes of that particular mission, be deputized in the name of the sender and in that event will appear on the planet of assignment with the full authority of the Bright and Morning Star. Especially is this true on those spheres where a higher Son has not yet appeared in the likeness of the creatures of the realm." *(Paper 35, Section 2, Para 3, 4)*

And it was this same Melchizedek, in recruiting and teaching the brilliant leader Abraham, who would later go forth and establish the Hebrew religion.

Melchizedek's teachings, as he sent his missionaries out to carry the message beyond Mesopotamia, became the foundation of almost every major world religion.

The Urantia Book dedicates six papers narrating his long-lasting influence found today in *Judaism, Christianity, Buddhism, Hinduism, Confucianism, Zoroastrianism* and later, *Islam*; for all have at their basic core of teaching a one-*God* or one-*Truth* concept.

And so in our own history, one such son known as *Machiventa Melchizedek* found his way into our historical records by conducting an *emergency mission* of keeping truth alive in the hearts and minds of early man:

"It is nearly four thousand years since this emergency Son of Nebadon bestowed himself on Urantia, and in that time the teachings of the "priest of El Elyon, the Most High God," have penetrated to all races and peoples. And Machiventa was successful in achieving the purpose of his unusual bestowal; when Michael made ready to appear on Urantia, the God concept was existent in the hearts of men and women, the same God concept that still flames anew in the living spiritual experience of the manifold children of the Universal Father as they live their intriguing temporal lives on the whirling planets of space." (Paper 98, Section 7, Para 12)

9 MICHAEL

Michael is the one and only Creator Son of our vast *local* universe, he is a direct offspring of *God the Father*, a personal and original expression of the Father and the Eternal Son (the first and second persons of Trinity):

"Each Creator Son is the only-begotten and only-begettable offspring of the perfect union of the original concepts of the two infinite and eternal and perfect minds of the ever-existent Creators of the universe of universes. There never can be another such Son because each Creator Son is the unqualified, finished, and final expression and embodiment of all of every phase of every feature of every possibility of every divine reality that could, throughout all eternity, ever be found in, expressed by, or evolved from, those divine creative potentials which united to bring this Michael Son into existence. Each Creator Son is the absolute of the united deity concepts which constitute his divine origin." (Paper 21, Section 1)

Michael, the most divine being (aside from God the Father) that we can ever know, is one and the same Jesus, the Son of Man and the Son of God; son of the Heavenly Father, incarnate in human form:

"It is of record that the divine Son of last appearance on your planet was a Paradise Creator Son who had completed six phases of his bestowal career; consequently, when he gave up the

conscious grasp of the incarnated life on Urantia, he could, and did, truly say, "It is finished" — it was literally finished. His death on Urantia completed his bestowal career; it was the last step in fulfilling the sacred oath of a Paradise Creator Son. And when this experience has been acquired, such Sons are supreme universe sovereigns; no longer do they rule as vicegerents of the Father but in their own right and name as "King of Kings and Lord of Lords." With certain stated exceptions these sevenfold bestowal Sons are unqualifiedly supreme in the universes of their abode. Concerning his local universe, "all power in heaven and on earth" was relegated to this triumphant and enthroned Master Son." (Paper 21, Section 4)

The Urantia Book explains that Michael (prior to physical incarnation) *chose our world* to accomplish what is called a **bestowal mission**. Such bestowals allow divine Sons' of such a high spiritual order to live and experience first-hand, the successive levels of existence. Michael started at the top, ending last, on this world as an evolutionary human being of the realm.

It is because "nothing in the universe can take the place of actual living experience," that such bestowals are undertaken. These bestowals also allow the Creator Son to personally reveal himself to the spiritual children as they exist on the successive levels throughout the universe. It is this two-fold purpose of bringing God to created personalities and of bringing those very children of the Creator to the Father, firsthand. This was his primary mission when he came to our world two-thousand years ago.

What better method could there be for this Creator Son to personally experience every phases of his creation than to actually live it as one himself among the creatures? What greater experience could a father have than to know the experience of his children-because he actually lived it with and through them, as one of them?

Jesus said, "He who has seen me has seen the Father." Jesus also said, "I come to live among you, but I have sheep of another flock."

Clearly, Jesus was attempting to express how he and the Father were one, and that he was a personal representation of the Father. The "sheep of another flock," was a way of saying that beyond the scope of physical life, Jesus also acknowledged his leadership role in the spiritual realm.

A better illustration of what the varying levels of reality are, as they are laid out in the Revelation, can best be shown by summation of the seven bestowals the divine or Creator Son must experience, from highest to lowest: In each bestowal, the Son exists in that realm, for a period of time.

In his successive bestowals, Michael lived as an individual of that realm in the following way:

First Bestowal: A Melchezidek Son. He served among them and with them for a period of about one hundred years, in which time he served on twenty-four missions of emergency service throughout the universe. This occurrence was said to have happen some one billion years ago.

Second bestowal: A Lanonandek Son. During a seventeen year time period, this Bestowal mission involved the appearing Son serving as a temporary System Sovereign of a system of worlds that had gone into rebellion (not unlike our own system when Lucifer rebelled) Michael as a System Sovereign, restored the system of worlds and adjudicated those who had led the worlds astray.

Third Bestowal: A Material Son. Again, Michael bestowed himself as a Material Son who served on an evolutionary world that had also been affected by rebellion. As Adam and Eve appeared on our world some 37,000 years ago, so did this Michael, in his desire to experience creation through bestowal, appear as a Material Son to restore order on a far distant world until a permanent Adam and Eve could arrive. As a Material Son, Michael served his incarnated life for an entire generation.

Fourth Bestowal: As Seraphim. Michael appeared in his new incarnated form and served as a seraphic angelic helper for a period of forty years. In this time, he assisted on twenty-two different worlds.

The Revelators state that at the times of each incarnation or appearance, it was not generally known by the inhabitants of each respective realm where or what Michael would appear as. Nor did the fellow associates know for sure that the appearing personality was in fact, the Creator Michael Son in incarnated form. All that was known at the time of each bestowal is that Michael would take absence from his rule of divine Creator Son for a season, then some years later, resume his seat as the spiritual ruler of the universe, but as a Creator Son who had completed a specific bestowal as a personality of the realm, as an individual personality specific to that level of existence.

Fifth Bestowal: An Ascendant Mortal named "Eventod." Michael served for eleven years as an ascendant mortal on a world where pilgrim mortals ascend prior to elevation to spirit status. The Revelators state that with this bestowal, it became evident that the remaining bestowals would be that of the Creator Son incarnating himself to that of the status of an evolutionary mortal. Not much is said regarding the specifics of what Eventod performed, but that his incarnation was a "This first appearance of Michael incarnated in the role of one stage of mortal evolution was an event which thrilled and enthralled all," since it was the first time such an incarnation occurred.

Sixth Bestowal: A Morontia Mortal. Michael's incarnation of that of a recently ascendant citizen in Morontian form allowed the Creator Son to experience life as it is lived in the realm just beyond the grasp of mortal understanding, that is to say, he assumed the type of being in the same form we as humans are to encounter when we translate from the death of the flesh, to the next phase of living existence as Morontia beings (physical, yet not completely spirit). He was known as Edantum; a Morontia mortal of evolutionary ascension.

Seventh Bestowal: Jesus of Nazareth. This was his last incarnation, and it afforded Michael the final experience to live life as a human being on an evolutionary world. For thirty-three years, Jesus lived among men, learned their ways, suffered and enjoyed living as we live life. Upon his death, Jesus (Michael) resurrected back to "the bosom of the Father," thus completing the mandate of experiencing each and all phases of existence, even as he, the Creator Son, sets forth for all of us to follow. As we will ascend to experience various levels of existence, Michael descended those very same levels, and in doing so, experienced life from every perspective from top to bottom.

The above summary of the seven bestowals not only portray the successive levels Michael attained in actual experience, but it also portrays something of how the ascension and progressive plane of spiritual growth actually works. I believe the Revelators sought to help us understand the varying levels of existence by narrating something of the bestowal experience. In this way we could grasp the ascension plan as being one of ever-progressive steps. In this way, the human mind can begin to contemplate how mortal life is but one phase of existence, in actuality, the first spiritual phase of a series that leads towards God and of Paradise. Just as Michael descended from the top going down, we as mortals of spiritual ascension, move upward and inward towards our Father on Paradise.

Wisdom, intellectual development, maturity of insight and growth of personal character are all earmarks of the experience of progressive living. Even a perfected Creator Son must go through the experience of living among his created beings in order to gain their insight. No living being in the universe is allowed to circumvent the process of actual experience; no living person can progress unless they actually learn by the process of doing it for him or herself. Wisdom comes through intellectual and spiritual application; one must learn by living.

This truth of living experience forever shatters the commonly held belief that we automatically become settled beings of light once our world here ends in death, and for this reason alone, the Revelation crosses a major threshold, because for the first time, a concept is being introduced that says we are all personally responsible for the gains we make, not only in this life, but in the next, and the next. No one can keep us from achieving spiritual growth; it is not handed to us freely, it is given to us because we yearn and desire to find it.

It is this everlasting partnership, as Jesus fully revealed in his life, between a father and his child, that involves the child reaching for perfection, and a father who leads the way.

10 THE BETTER ANGELS OF OUR NATURE

"There are three distinct orders of the personalities of the Infinite Spirit. The impetuous apostle understood this when he wrote respecting Jesus, "who has gone to heaven and is on the right hand of God, angels and authorities and powers being made subject to him. "Angels are the ministering spirits of time; authorities, the messenger hosts of space; powers, the higher personalities of the Infinite Spirit." (Paper 38, Section 1)

Most people might have a particularly hard time with the concept of angels (especially in the modern age). A lot of people casually believe they exist, many books have been written about them and there is no shortage of literature concerning their natures. Our theological history incorporates them without end and even non-religious people are fond of the notion of their existence, but few are able to explain angels, who they are and what they actually do:

"Angels do not have material bodies, but they are definite and discrete beings; they are of spirit nature and origin. Though invisible to mortals, they perceive you as you are in the flesh without the aid of transformers or translators; they intellectually understand the mode of mortal life, and they share all of man's non-sensuous emotions and sentiments. They appreciate and

greatly enjoy your efforts in music, art, and real humor. They are fully cognizant of your moral struggles and spiritual difficulties. They love human beings, and only good can result from your efforts to understand and love them.

Though seraphim are very affectionate and sympathetic beings, they are not sex-emotion creatures. They are much as you will be on the mansion worlds, where you will "neither marry nor be given in marriage but will be as the angels of heaven." For all who " shall be accounted worthy to attain the mansion worlds neither marry nor are given in marriage; neither do they die any more, for they are equal to the angels. " Nevertheless, in dealing with sex creatures it is our custom to speak of those beings of more direct descent from the Father and the Son as the sons of God, while referring to the children of the Spirit as the daughters of God. Angels are, therefore, commonly designated by feminine pronouns on the sex planets." (Paper 38, Section 2)

The Revelation claims they are all around us and accomplish much for us. They are here to help us, but they certainly don't spend their time catering to our every need:

"The seraphim are so created as to function on both spiritual and literal levels. There are few phases of morontia or spirit activity which are not open to their ministrations. While in personal status angels are not so far removed from human beings, in certain functional performances seraphim far transcend them. They possess many powers far beyond human comprehension. For example: You have been told that the "very hairs of your head are numbered," and it is true they are, but a seraphim does not spend her time counting them and keeping the number corrected up to date. Angels possess inherent and automatic (that is, automatic as far as you could perceive) powers of knowing such things; you would truly regard a seraphim as a mathematical prodigy. Therefore, numerous duties which would be tremendous tasks for mortals are performed with exceeding ease by seraphim.

Angels are superior to you in spiritual status, but they are not your judges or accusers. No matter what your faults, "the angels, although greater in power and might, bring no accusation against you. "Angels do not sit in judgment on mankind; neither should individual mortals prejudge their fellow creatures.

You do well to love them, but you should not adore them; angels are not objects of worship. The great seraphim, Loyalatia, when your seer "fell down to worship before the feet of the angel," said: " See that you do it not; I am a fellow servant with you and with your races, who are all enjoined to worship God."

In nature and personality endowment the seraphim are just a trifle ahead of mortal races in the scale of creature existence. Indeed, when you are delivered from the flesh, you become very much like them. On the mansion worlds you will begin to appreciate the seraphim, on the constellation spheres to enjoy them, while on Salvington (the headquarters of our Local Universe) they will share their places of rest and worship with you. Throughout the whole morontia and subsequent spirit ascent, your fraternity with the seraphim will be ideal; your companionship will be superb." (Paper 38, Section 2)

As human beings, it is our job to gain the valuable experience of living with faith and always with our eye on the moral and ethical ball. Angels, it would appear, also need living experience, for "nothing in the universe takes the place of experience," as angels are required (just like us on the material level) to learn from the daily experience of living. The Revelation gives a plethora of information on their natures and purpose.

As mentioned in earlier chapters of this writing, according the Revelators, the universe is cared for by personalities from the highest spiritual order of existence to the lowest order. Angels are "born" through the third person of Deity, the *Infinite Spirit*; angels are her offspring as *Sons of God* are the spiritual offspring of God the Father. For example, Jesus would be an offspring of the *Second Person of Deity*, while say, your "guardian angel" would be of a nature and offspring of the Holy Spirit.

While institutionalized religion is not short on sermon, very little is known regarding the varying degrees between God, angels and men. The Revelation seeks to differentiate between the commonly held views between the varying levels of spiritual life and spiritual personalities who exist in this realm

To illustrate my point, notice the hierarchy of the military: Generals are at the top, but at the bottom working their way up, we see 2nd Lieutenants, 1st Lieutenants, Captains, Majors, Lt. Colonels, Colonels and finally Generals, and within these, levels of rank ascend from Brigadier, Major, Lieutenant and finally General General (those are the ones with four stars).

To most civilians an officer is an officer, but a military person knows the difference between a *Captain* and a *General-* and there is a big difference. To take this illustration a little further, rank distinguishes command or areas of responsibility. Generals command entire divisions, Captains might be in charge of one regiment or command post or even a flight. While rank designates level of authority as well as responsibility, it also designates experience.

Similarly, The Revelation designates spiritual personalities by their rank-or administrative responsibility. A Son of God is a very high-ranking personality, but within each Son class, there are designates like "Material Son," "Creator Son," or a "Life Carrier Son," descriptive terms of what they do with regard to universal affairs.

It appears to be the same with angels. The book details exhaustively that there are high ranking seraphim and low ranking seraphim. In fact, much of the first and second parts of the Revelation are dedicated to explaining just what everyone does in the universe. It would appear than in every function, in every phase and covering all aspects of cosmological function, every order of personality has within it, ascending orders of rank and responsibility.

God is at the top, followed by the Trinity, followed by each expressive personality of that triune relationship, followed by offspring Sons, offspring of the Infinite Spirit, angelic orders and so on, ending with man at the lowest level. We comprise the lowest type of spiritual expression (in that we possess soul potential), but also represent the highest form of material life (because we possess spirit).

It would appear that for the first time, we are given specific information as to the rank and file of an entire universe. It would appear, according to the Revelators, the universe is very orderly.

In current theology, there is almost no distinction between what God is and what angels are; between what God does and what angels do. To the common person raised in any church in middle-America, God does everything and angels seem to have nothing but time on their hands to help us get out of crisis and answer every prayer we can utter.

This kind of religious depth leaves very little to contemplate- and what's worse is we are told from the very beginning (by our church leaders) that this is all we need to know. The level of theological understanding in the modern age remains somewhat shallow, owing to the fact that much of our religious teaching comes from the very pages of what was learned and taught over a thousand years ago. Imagine learning math the same way we did in 5 A.D. and being told there was nothing more to learn. This is our religion instruction. The Revelators clearly state, "*the time has come to make frank statements*" about reality.

Angels are designated by many names, each of which denotes a *level of experience or inherent ability*. For example, Cherubim are fairly inexperienced (and also have different destinies than Seraphim). Seconaphim would be a trifle more experienced than Seraphim; Supernaphim would be the highest, or most experienced of them all.

Angels are created uniformly, and in large groups at a time. The differing natures are in part due to the purposes for which they were produced and in the experience they acquire through actual living and working in their respective careers. As they gain experience their spiritual ability becomes ever-more acute; their wise counsel becomes more sought after, their administrative duty and level of responsibility becomes greater in the grand scheme of spiritual affairs.

Many of our funniest movies depicting fallen angels who are required to come back and save some poor soul are in actuality, not far off the mark.

As human beings, we are given the task of raising children. Much of what we do for them is seldom understood or observed by our children as they grow. Children live in an ever-present reality, they move from thought to thought without much regard for the future or the past. As parents, it is our job to insure their safety and to guide them along their way, always ready to help them, but also cognizant of the more important duty of teaching them how to behave and take care of themselves. As the father of three, I recognize it to be my role to administer to their well-being and character development, but not to prevent them from learning to fix their mistakes or allow them to fail from time to time so that lessons can be learned. The symmetry of being a parent is that while my children grow older in knowledge of how to live their lives, so do I gain wisdom by teaching them what I have learned during my own life.

In this same way, angels are portrayed as being our guides. The parallels are the same; parents gain wisdom by teaching their young, the young gain knowledge and become more to their potential by the guidance they receive from us, the better teachers we are, the better (and more fulfilled) children we raise.

To angels, we are their spiritual children (or cousins). It is their job to work side by side with us, in the shadows so to speak, and as we gain knowledge on the affairs of living in this world, so do they learn how to be more effective as spiritual instructors. It's a simplified observation, but the Revelators say it is further proof of an intelligently guided universe premised on cooperation and service.

The Revelation says angels lack but one vital element that we possess, and that is *faith in the unseen.*

Angels have a spiritual origin, they hail from a spiritual source, and their existence begins already in spiritual form. Humans exist in the material world; we are called to believe in something that cannot be proven at least by material senses. With faith, we exhibit willingness and a trust to believe in something we cannot see. This exhibition of material-minded faith carries great weight in the cosmos; it is unmatched and it is a display of spiritual courage all other beings of high order would love the opportunity to display-if they could.

Showing a willingness to hold out hope is the passing of the ultimate human test. Having faith is what makes ascendant human beings distinctively different from our animal cousins as well as our spiritual ones.

The odds are stacked against us. It is expected many of us will fail to live up to the test of faith. Like parents who work diligently to insure their offspring are guided along the right path, so do angels work heroically to guide their human cousins to seek out spiritual answers in a material world.

But not all angels are assigned to the watch care of human beings.

Seraphic personalities are found to be involved in almost every facet of universe function, from assisting high spiritual personalities with the administering of super-universe affairs; transporting personalities from one location of the universe to another; recording and making available historical events of record; broadcasting information from one part of the galaxy to another; these are some of the duties seraphic personalities perform.. Seraphic hosts are the helpers who keep the universe moving forward.

Here at home, Seraphic personalities, by designate, are listed as follows:

The Spirits of Brotherhood: These angels work to bring the races together, the coordinate effort "behind the scenes" to promote universal brotherhood and racial harmony.

The Souls of Peace: Angels who coordinate efforts to help men find peace and to promote resolution in the face of conflict among governments.

The Spirits of Trust: Angels whose job it is to "inculcate trust" in the human mind and among generations of men, to work towards the development of trust among cultures and varying peoples.

The Transporters: They are charged with bringing visitors to and from our world, students or personalities who come from Jerusem and back, including the many student visitors who communicated with Sadler for over 30 years.

The Recorders: Those angels are commissioned to record the world events down through the ages, many of whom were of great assistance in compiling the narrative of the Revelation.

Here is but one description from the Urantia Book which describes angelic function in escorting a being from his earthly estate:

"Your conventional idea of angels has been derived in the following way: During moments just prior to physical death a reflective phenomenon sometimes occurs in the human mind, and this dimming consciousness seems to visualize something of the form of the attending angel, and this is immediately translated into terms of the habitual concept of angels held in that individual's mind.

The erroneous idea that angels possess wings is not wholly due to olden notions that they must have wings to fly through the air. Human beings have sometimes been permitted to observe seraphim that were being prepared for transport service, and the traditions of these experiences have largely determined the Urantian concept of angels. In observing a transport seraphim being made ready to receive a passenger for interplanetary transit, there may be seen what are apparently double sets of wings extending from the head to the foot of the angel. In reality these wings are energy insulators—friction shields.

When celestial beings are to be enseraphimed for transfer from one world to another, they are brought to the headquarters of the sphere and, after due registry, are inducted into the transit sleep. Meantime, the transport seraphim moves into a horizontal position immediately above the universe energy pole of the planet. While the energy shields are wide open, the sleeping personality is skillfully deposited, by the officiating seraphic assistants, directly on top of the transport angel. Then both the upper and lower pairs of shields are carefully closed and adjusted.

And now, under the influence of the transformers and the transmitters, a strange metamorphosis begins as the seraphim is made ready to swing into the energy currents of the universe circuits. To outward appearance the seraphim grows pointed at both extremities and becomes so enshrouded in a queer light of amber hue that very soon it is impossible to distinguish the enseraphimed personality. When all is in readiness for departure, the chief of transport makes the proper inspection of the carriage of life, carries out the routine tests to ascertain whether or not the angel is properly encircuited, and then announces that the traveler is properly enseraphimed, that the energies are adjusted, that the angel is insulated, and that everything is in readiness for the departing flash. The mechanical controllers, two of them, next take their positions. By this time the transport seraphim has become an almost transparent, vibrating, torpedo-shaped outline of glistening luminosity. Now the transport dispatcher of the realm summons the auxiliary batteries of the living energy transmitters, usually one thousand in number; as he announces the destination of the transport, he reaches out and touches the near point of the seraphic carriage, which shoots forward with lightninglike speed, leaving a trail of celestial luminosity as far as the planetary atmospheric investment extends. In less than ten minutes the marvelous spectacle will be lost even to reinforced seraphic vision." (Paper 39, Section 5)

Angels work in pairs, and from what the Revelation says about their works with individuals, they are supervisory over groups of people as well. For example, they monitor large groups of individuals, instilling challenges and fostering intelligent cooperation among them; *they assist in bringing like-minded individual together.*

Angels inspire insight and manipulate conditions so as to provoke growth through wisdom. In times of peaceful rumination, it is said they encourage worshipful feelings.

Angels have a colorful history and are interwoven into our psyche, as they appear in man's oldest records.

Of angels it is said we should trust them to be our guiding teachers through our life in the flesh. Only good can come from understanding them, the Revelators say, appreciation of their presence builds a trusting confidence between us and our unseen cousins in the spirit.

Most of us (including myself) can look back on a moment in our lives and point to an unexplained event where angelic forces might have intervened. We can't prove our suspicions, but we know in our hearts something unexplained might have occurred.

Whether it was a life or death situation, a sudden choosing to turn left instead of right, a feeling of certainty that luck came at the exact moment it shouldn't have, or even a light or apparition that inspired us in our darkest hour, we have all felt a brush of supernatural kindness or influence. And so, assuming for the sake of argument that angels do exist, let me share additional information as it is presented in the celestial text concerning angels and their interaction with their mortal cousins in the flesh.

By their nature angels are either negatively or positively charged, one retreating, one aggressive, *left* and *right,* if you will, capable of manipulating environment (without violating the laws of nature). It is the job of any guardian angels to help us see more effectively with spiritual clarity, to make decision based on altruistic impulses instead of self-centered ones. The capacity for a human being to become influenced by ones' guiding seraphic associate depends very much on our willingness to follow our impulse to do good or to seek truth in any given decision.

It is not the job of angels to bring ease to our life, so says the Urantia Book.

Difficulties challenge us and force us to put effort into our thinking process. The correlation between angels and parents are strikingly similar, in almost every example of a good parenting skills, one can see the same method being employed by angels.

Consider the following passage on the subject of the purpose of angelic assistance

Do we grant every wish our child makes?
Do we honor hard work and effort?

Do we watch over our children, but allow them to make mistakes?
Do we do everything we can to inspire knowledge and insight?
Do we expect them to learn for themselves?
Do we pamper them in excess or do we create an atmosphere that will instill strong character?

It is stated that the higher up the ladder an angel ascends on the spiritual level of existence, the more they petition to be assigned to the worst of circumstance on an evolutionary world, ever seeking an opportunity to assist those in the greatest of need.

This desire among angels to work with those most in need illustrates the angelic desire to go as low as possible in order to gain the highest experience. If angels desire to do this, then it must be in their nature to inspire us to do the same.

The Revelation says of angels that as they understand us and seek to offer us guidance, and as they sympathize with our struggles of mortal living, we should come to know and trust them, even to understand their natures so as to gain a better appreciation of their work.

Of angels it is said they enjoy our humor and they enjoy our achievements, similarly, the share delight in our artistic expression. They are patient and they reckon time in expressions of eternity; they perceive long-term accomplishments and are not frustrated by short-term failure.

Angels can forecast likelihood of events, predict pattern of human behavior and anticipate outcome. As previously mentioned, they are mathematical geniuses and have the ability to "know" what is transpiring outside of their immediate presence because of the inter-connective communication with others of their kind. They are extremely effective in getting people together in the effort to accomplish the greatest good for the greatest number of individuals involved. Whether it is local, regional or global, when catastrophe strikes, angels can be counted to help us maintain order and prevent societal breakdown.

Angels, as they are portrayed in the Revelation, seem to be custodians, guardians, liaisons, and effective coordinators of planetary our affairs. It is said, *"the Most Highs rule in the kingdom of men."*

A phrase that is becoming quite popular in society is "positive energy." People who are on a spiritual path are said to focus on "positive energy." It is the fervent wish of the Revelators to have a better understanding of the forces and agents who work for our behalf, and if this "positive energy" is in fact the spiritual force that works in concert with our goal "to be perfect," then I would submit that angels are definitely "positive energy," in that they work for those things which are true, good and beautiful.

11 LIFE AFTER DEATH

The following excerpt is how the Revelators describe what happens to us when we awake from mortal death:

"On the mansion worlds the resurrected mortal survivors resume their lives just where they left off when overtaken by death.

When you go from Urantia to the first mansion world, you will notice considerable change, but if you had come from a more normal and progressive sphere of time, you would hardly notice the difference except for the fact that you were in possession of a different body; the tabernacle of flesh and blood has been left behind on the world of nativity.

From the Temple of New Life there extend seven radial wings, the resurrection halls of the mortal races. Each of these structures is devoted to the assembly of one of the seven races of time. There are one hundred thousand personal resurrection chambers in each of these seven wings terminating in the circular class assembly halls, which serve as the awakening chambers for as many as one million individuals. These halls are surrounded by the personality assembly chambers of the blended races of the normal post-Adamic worlds. Regardless of the technique which may be employed on the individual worlds of time in connection with special or dispensational resurrections, the real and conscious reassembly of actual and complete personality takes place in the resurrection halls of mansonia number one. Throughout all eternity you will recall the profound memory impressions of your first witnessing of these resurrection mornings." (Paper 47, Section 3, Para 1, 5)

The common misconception among contemporary theological belief is that, when a human being dies, we go *suddenly* from being a mortal, animalistic type of creation, to a being of spirit perfection; that with death from the material, we are suddenly transformed to a being of spiritual light, to an almost angelic type of being.

Not so say the Revelators, who state that the bridge between mortal imperfection and spiritual perfection involves not one, but many transformations:

"When the Creators desire to produce perfect beings, they do so by direct and original creation, but they never undertake to convert animal-origin and material creatures into beings of perfection in a single step...

...What magic could death, the natural dissolution of the material body, hold that such a simple step should instantly transform the mortal and material mind into an immortal and perfected spirit? Such beliefs are but ignorant superstitions and pleasing fables...

...Between the time of planetary death or translation and resurrection on the mansion world, mortal man gains absolutely nothing aside from experiencing the fact of survival. You begin over there right where you leave off down here."

In the Urantia Book, the actual process goes something like this. All human beings contain within them a fragment of the Father's spirit, and we also possess identity (or personality) that makes us uniquely different from one another. These two non-material entities are all that remain of us after mortal death. Our identity and our spirit fragment as two separate and distinct entities are rejoined on what is called *The Mansion World*.

The *Mansion Worlds* are known as transition spheres - or planets. There are fifty-six spheres that revolve the headquarters world known as *Jerusem*.

The Revelators are point out the term Jesus used to describe his Fathers Heavenly place, "In my father's house are many *mansions*," thus the term "mansion" was deliberately chosen by the Revelators because they wanted to be specific to the term - *as Jesus himself used*. Since our theological language contained the word symbol, the Revelators saw fit to use it.

We are resurrected on the Mansion Worlds, provided forms or bodies made of a substance called *Morontia*, which the papers describe as consisting of material elements made up of *exactly double* the number of elements found on evolutionary worlds, as well as other forms of energy patterns not revealed to us. The papers go into great detail how *morontia material* is a *liaison phase* of energy that exists between material and spirit.

The Revelators quote Paul the Apostle who, when describing this liaison material said, *"they have in heaven a better and more enduring substance,"* a material manipulated, controlled and regulated by beings are who are themselves, made of this substance:

"Paul learned of the existence of the morontia worlds and of the reality of morontia materials, for he wrote, "They have in heaven a better and more enduring substance. "And these morontia materials are real, literal, even as in "the city which has foundations, whose builder and maker is God. "And each of these marvelous spheres is "a better country, that is, a heavenly one." (Paper 48, Section 1, Para. 7)

Hence, our life on the Mansion World is called *The Morontia Life*.

When we are resurrected from the "sleep of death," that is to say, when our identity-personality and the spirit fragment of God are brought into union into this new body form, we are welcomed in these resurrection halls by a Morontia Companion who is designated as a *Pilgrim Receiver*, *"whose duty it will be to introduce you to the world you have just been received."*

It should also be noted that resurrections usually occur at the end of a dispensation of a planetary age; the last one occurring when Christ was resurrected some two thousand years ago. The periodic en masse resurrections are conducted so that all human beings who have died a physical death over a period of an age, are resurrected *at the same time* - and that in death, the passing of time is of no consequence. The reason stated for periodic resurrection is because it is much more efficient to resurrect large groups who have similar references in culture, language and evolutionary development.

Evolutionary beings that have passed from mortal life from their other native worlds all first come to these Mansion Worlds. These worlds are the first step for all surviving mortals, the first step for many on a long journey inward toward Paradise, the physical dwelling place of God at the center of the Universe of Universes.

Once resurrected, the unique experience of personality survival is said to be quite overwhelming, so much so that *Morontia Companions* (beings of an angelic type, but who are visible) serve as counselors, instructors and mediators who help us come to terms with our new existence.

One fascinating statement in the Revelation has to do with the description of how, when we are first resurrected, our earthly existence will seem much like a dream, but over time memories of our earth life will become clarified, in much the same way we might reflect upon our younger years of early life as children while still in the flesh.

The papers go on to describe the types of personalities who administer the Mansion worlds, consisting of Cherubim, Sanobim, Morontia Companions, Mansion World Teachers, Melchizedeks, and Celestial Artisans.

It is stated that as we ascend personality development, our spiritual vision becomes acute, and with each passing phase (or transformation) higher spirit personalities become more visible to us. Mansion Worlds are inhabited by ascending mortals of the realm as well as spiritual beings who are literal custodians of the sphere, supervisors who maintain government relations, administer social function and instruct newly resurrected beings in the ways, language and culture of this first transition world.

The first Mansion World (of which there are seven, and reminiscent of the term "*seventh heaven*") is very similar in function to a world we might envision as a utopia of the future. It is physical, it has rivers and lakes, water, plant life (a botanical paradise by our standards) places of residents, societies, cities, centers of worship, centers of culture and study, a veritable new world, but with the cohabitation of ascending mortals of time as well as permanent angelic-like personalities of eternity.

Our early ascendant life on the Mansion World is dedicated at first, to learning the language (though we will still speak our own native language) and *un*learning the negative behavioral habits we acquired while growing up on an evolutionary world. Personality and character development is taught in order to eliminate the earthly tendencies like greed, extreme self-centeredness, jealousy, envy, prejudice and procrastination.

There is a tremendous amount of "rehabilitation" offered to the individual in order to allow more effective and cooperative development with others in the social setting now existent on this new place we call home. Much of our and sojourn on this first Mansion World is spent helping us adjust to living among others in peace so that real spiritual understanding can be achieved. There are schools of conduct, schools of language, schools of philosophy and schools of mind and character development. More emphasis is put on character development, on how to interact with others and how to improve ourselves so that we can continue onward in this plan of universal ascension.

With each level attained, transformations occur within is that allow us to "see" spiritual truth more clearly; our vision becomes more spiritual and less material. Higher types of spiritual beings become visible to us as we ascend in mind and personality development, our ability to feel the presence of the Universal Father within becomes more acute during these times of education on the Mansion Worlds. We are *ascendant* beings, and since time is now lived from *the eternal point of view*, instead of the finite perspective, a different set of values is soon realized.

Physically, we still exist on a material world, but we are introduced to spiritual realities and philosophy intended to help us grow spiritually, as well as intellectually. The Revelators say many of the higher forms of recreation activity found in more modern societies (on more progressive evolutionary worlds) exist also on the Mansion world, including concerts, performances and even competitive games.

We retain our male or female attributes throughout our existence, though we cease to be *sexually* productive. The Revelators state, *"Many orders of universe creatures are created in dual phases of personality manifestation,"* aggressive and retiring, male and female - whatever the designation, it is ours to keep and will remain a part of our natures throughout our universe career. The reason for this dual-phase is that *"such dual associations greatly multiply versatility and overcome inherent limitations."*

The attributes of aggressive and retiring types of personalities work well together throughout creation.

Another facet of the post-earth existence is the pre-requisite of *parenting.* The celestial authors point out that *raising of offspring is a requirement of all ascendant personalities*; all people must gain the experience of being a parent.

If, upon death, one does not have this experience, they are destined to gain this experience by either raising children they may have prematurely lost while on earth (children who met with an early death), or we will assist as guardians of other children whose parents may not have attained personality survival. We are all required to have the experience of raising children through the pubescent age.

It is the divine plan that ascendant beings gain the parental experience - God wants everyone to share in this experience (pause to the consider the possibility that those parents who so tragically lost their loved ones on earth are now going to be given a chance to raise those very children in the next life. This statement is perhaps one of the most delightful messages of hope contained in the whole revelatory text):

"And it is one of the most touchingly beautiful scenes of all the ascending career to observe the mansion world parents embrace their material offspring on the occasions of their periodic pilgrimages. While one or both parents may leave a mansion

world ahead of the child, they are quite often contemporary for a season." (Paper 47, Section 1, Para. 5)

Personality survival is dependent on one factor alone; **the willingness to believe in something greater than ourselves.** As said Jesus, "it is your faith that saves you."

It is said that if and *only* when a mortal repeatedly rejects the notion of spiritual reality, and if they reject this notion to a point where no spiritual possibility can exist within the mind of that person, it is by *their* choice that determines their survival beyond mortal existence.

If it is determined by the *adjudicators*, or spirit personalities who review the identity of each individual who passes through mortal death, that such an individual displayed (within their own mind) a consistent rejection of the notion of a spiritual or religious impulse, then upon death, the personality of the individual is extinguished *as if he never was*, only his memories remain, which are carried back to the Universal Father (God) with the spirit fragment that was part of the persons' life during his existence as a mortal evolutionary being. In other words, one would have to commit to his or her mind a fervent belief *against* faith, in order to extinguish from him or her the hope of soul survival.

The Revelators also say the spiritual life actually initiates on earth once a person accepts the notion that he or she is indwelt with the living spirit of God, then one does not need to wait until he or she arrives resurrected on a Mansion world to begin his or hers' spiritual development. The mere fact of reawakening on a Mansion world in a newly formed body does not in the least bit devalue the importance of living a spiritual life in the flesh. In truth, one's level of growth is all the more determined by their consecration and dedication to being *good* and *true* while still a mortal evolutionary being.

The same can be said that while in the flesh, if one is more dedicated to selfishness and self-centeredness while living out their life on earth, it will only take away from their eventual progress and advancement in ascending up through the various stages of existence after one survives death on the Mansion Worlds. It is always *your* choice. Your destiny is ultimately *up to you*.

Other interesting details contained pertaining to life after death include the variety of personalities who exist, including *Reversion Directors*, those who might be analogous to comedians and entertainers. Celestial Artisan are capable of presenting plays and recreating epochal events, present wondrous performances beyond anything we can even imagine, utilizing ensembles of not just thousands of performers, but tens of thousands.

Music is described as not just sound, but the utilization of multiple senses, and harmonies that causes the listener to experience spiritual sensations beyond anything we've ever experienced before. Social recreation is of high value on the Mansion worlds.

Individually, the Revelators say, we have careers that match all of our earthly endeavors and beyond. Life on the Mansion Worlds will be comprised of work, study, social interaction with ascendant beings and other spirit personalities of a realm.

The weather on the Mansion Worlds is well-nigh near perfect; the average temperature is between 55 and 75 degrees. Because of the settled and comfortable environment, living dwellings are not generally covered.

Since the worlds are architecturally "made-to-order" in the sense that they are settled spheres, they consist of the same heavier elements found on most sun orbiting satellites, but they also include, as mentioned earlier, elements and variations of elements that do not exist on evolutionary spheres.

Hurricanes, storms and other destructive phenomena do not occur, as there are lakes, but no vast oceans that contribute to the erratic weather phenomena.

Methods of travel are with types of vehicles that use "energy streams," (though what energy streams might be are not revealed). There is also a mention of transport birds that are large enough to provide beings with transit.

Not much is said about commerce or even if there is a form of it, but it is stated we do work in occupations not dissimilar to our "worldly endeavors;" we do contribute and function within the social system that exists in the Morontia life.

The assumed theological belief is that heaven is a place where we simply exist in a state of bliss; it would appear that the Revelators wanted us to know otherwise. Life after death appears to be a continuation of what is initiated here on earth. Many times the author's state that *"you pick up there, where you left off here,"* ascendancy is gradual, only the resurrection itself and the experience of personality survival is sudden.

It may well be shocking to the average reader to think of heaven as anything less than a state of glorified bliss, only because it has always been taught to us that eternal life is the ultimate reward for having to put up with the trials and tribulations of earthly life.

If living amongst peoples from other worlds, sharing with old earth acquaintances the stories of a life lived and a life now living, all the while participating in a new life what is in store for us, then perhaps this revelatory presentation is not so hard to believe. In the words of Meredith Sprunger, a long time reader and United Church of Christ Minister who was one of the early promoters of the Urantia Book, "if this is not true, it should be, or it might be very close to what we conceive heaven to be."

The Revelation presents twenty-nine pages to the narrative of the immediate life on the Mansion Worlds, and to the Morontia Life itself.

Consider the following passages on the ascendant life:

"The mortal-survival plan has a practical and serviceable objective; you are not the recipients of all this divine labor and painstaking training only that you may survive just to enjoy endless bliss and eternal ease. There is a goal of transcendent service concealed beyond the horizon of the present universe age. If God designed merely to take you on one long and eternal joy excursion, He certainly would not so largely turn the whole universe into one vast and intricate practical training school,

requisition a substantial part of the celestial creation as teachers and instructors, and then spend ages upon ages piloting you, one by one, through this gigantic universe school of experiential training. The furtherance of the scheme of mortal progression seems to be one of the chief businesses of the present organized universe, and the majority of innumerable orders of created intelligences are either directly or indirectly engaged in advancing some phase of this progressive perfection plan...."

"...In traversing the ascending scale of living existence from mortal man to the Deity embrace, you actually live the very life of every possible phase and stage of perfected creature existence within the limits of the present universe age...."

"...In the days of the mortal flesh the divine spirit indwells you, almost as a thing apart--in reality an invasion of man by the bestowed spirit of the Universal Father. But in the morontia life the spirit will become a real part of your personality, and as you successively pass through the 570 progressive transformations, you ascend from the material to the spiritual estate of creature life."

"...As you ascend the mansion worlds one by one, they become more crowded with the morontia activities of advancing survivors. As you go forward, you will recognize more and more of the Jerusem features added to the mansion worlds. The sea of glass makes its appearance on the second mansonia..."

"...John the Revelator saw a vision of the arrival of a class of advancing mortals from the seventh mansion world to their first heaven, the glories of Jerusem. He recorded: " And I saw as it were a sea of glass mingled with fire; and those who had gained the victory over the beast that was originally in them and over the image that persisted through the mansion worlds and finally over the last mark and trace, standing on the sea of glass, having the harps of God, and singing the song of deliverance from mortal fear and death... "

"...Paul also had a view of the ascendant-citizen corps of perfecting mortals on Jerusem, for he wrote: " But you have come to Mount Zion and to the city of the living God, the heavenly Jerusalem, and to an innumerable company of angels, to the grand *assembly of Michael, and to the spirits of just men being made perfect. " (Paper 47, Section 10)*

No doubt many people will be comforted by the concept of Heaven as it is presented in the Urantia Papers.

Since most of us have at one time or another pondered the question "is there life after death or is there really is a heaven?"

The Urantia Book boldly attempts to answer this most intriguing question – and with original detail perhaps never presented before to this extent.

12 THE HUMAN STORY OF JESUS

Jesus was all of the things the church portrays him to be; he loved all people, he laid down his life to show his dedication to his father, he walked the walk and he talked the talk. More than anything else, though, he was *human* as well as divine.

Jesus had three brothers and three sisters. When his father Joseph died because of a fall while helping to build a home in nearby Capernaum, Jesus, age 14, then had to help his mother Mary raise his young siblings. Their names were James, Joseph, Jude, Miriam, Martha and Ruth. Jesus' distant cousin was also John the Baptist, as Mary's was related to Elizabeth, the mother of John, according to The Urantia Book.

Life for the first several years after Joseph had passed away was extremely difficult both financially and emotionally for Jesus and his family. Prior to Joseph's death, the family had very high hopes for their eldest son Jesus, as he had displayed high intelligence, which indicated a promising scholarly career. And it was the plan of his parents to send Jesus off to the best schools in Jerusalem. Religious teachers of the day were extremely impressed by Jesus 'ability to grasp the rabbinic teachings,' his oratory skills were exemplary, and all of the neighbors were very fond of this boy from Nazareth, though no one for a moment (excepting his mother) suspected Jesus to be anything other than an exceptionally gifted young lad. No one treated Jesus any differently from other boys of his age, excepting that he was well liked. When one thinks of the glorified Christ, one forgets the human boy who was Jesus. The Revelators thought it important to tell his story, for history has forgotten that Jesus was a man long before the world began to think of him as a divine Redeemer:

"Before he was eight years of age, he was known to all the mothers and young women of Nazareth, who had met him and talked with him at the spring, which was not far from his home, and which was one of the social centers of contact and gossip for the entire town. This year Jesus learned to milk the family cow and care for the other animals. During this and the following year he also learned to make cheese and to weave. When he was ten years of age, he was an expert loom operator. It was about this time that Jesus and the neighbor boy Jacob became great friends of the potter who worked near the flowing spring; and as they watched Nathan's deft fingers mold the clay on the potter's wheel, many times both of them determined to be potters when they grew up. Nathan was very fond of the lads and often gave them clay to play with, seeking to stimulate their creative imaginations by suggesting competitive efforts in modeling various objects and animals." (Paper 115, Section 5, Para. 15)

Jesus painstakingly learned carpentry, became a skilled stonemason, taught himself to build boats, became an expert fisherman and learned the laws according to Moses as best anyone could. He was a Jewish boy growing up in a time when Rome ruled Judea and lived in much the same way as many other Jewish children of his time. There was nothing miraculous about Jesus other than (according to the Revelators) the fact that he was a divine son *incarnate* in the flesh, living the same life on this world as you and I would live. Jesus was not aware of his divinity during his youth, as the awareness of his divinity came much later as his mind become more cognizant of the spiritual voice within him.

During his later adolescence, Jesus helped to rear and teach his younger brothers and sisters. They were poor (which was somewhat common among Jewish families during the 1st

Century), but Jesus and Mary worked hard to maintain a close family. From the years from his mid-teens to his early late 20's, there were no miracles in Jesus' life, to the point where even Mary had doubted the vision of Gabriel, who told her she would bear a child of divine heritage.

There was however, a growing sense of realization within the mind of Jesus that he was more just a human being. Jesus was extremely dedicated to his worship and communion, he was devoted to the relationship he had with his spiritual Father and he grew keenly aware of his pre-existing status as a divine Creator.   This self-awareness increased on through early adulthood.

Like all men and woman, it was because of his determination to 'follow the Fathers' will' that such a deep spiritual relationship grew within Jesus' heart and mind.

Jesus did not become fully aware of his spiritual identity until the day of his baptism. Until that time, Jesus faced the same emotions, trial and tribulations as any other human being would. Jesus lived as a human being because he *was* a human being. Modern religion ignores this wonderful aspect of Jesus's personality, and thus many people who might otherwise find comfort relating to *the human Jesus* are redirected to the glorified Christ, while ignoring the other story; that a divine being was as human and real as you and me.

The Revelators presented the full view of Jesus' life because they wanted to give Jesus back to the people.

In the same way Jesus sought to bring God the Father to men and women in his time, as do the Revelators seek to present the narrative of this one time human being, who lived life among men as a man.

From Paper 196, on *The Faith of Jesus*:

"Jesus enjoyed a sublime and wholehearted faith in God. He experienced the ordinary ups and downs of mortal existence, but he never religiously doubted the certainty of God's watch care and guidance. His faith was the outgrowth of the insight born of the

activity of the divine presence, his indwelling Adjuster. His faith was neither traditional nor merely intellectual; it was wholly personal and purely spiritual.

The human Jesus saw God as being holy, just, and great, as well as being true, beautiful, and good. All these attributes of divinity he focused in his mind as the "will of the Father in heaven." Jesus' God was at one and the same time "The Holy One of Israel" and "The living and loving Father in heaven." The concept of God as a Father was not original with Jesus, but he exalted and elevated the idea into a sublime experience by achieving a new revelation of God and by proclaiming that every mortal creature is a child of this Father of love, a son of God.

"...Theology may fix, formulate, define, and dogmatize faith, but in the human life of Jesus faith was personal, living, original, spontaneous, and purely spiritual. This faith was not reverence for tradition nor a mere intellectual belief which he held as a sacred creed, but rather a sublime experience and a profound conviction which securely held him. His faith was so real and all-encompassing that it absolutely swept away any spiritual doubts and effectively destroyed every conflicting desire. Nothing was able to tear him away from the spiritual anchorage of this fervent, sublime, and undaunted faith. Even in the face of apparent defeat or in the throes of disappointment and threatening despair, he calmly stood in the divine presence free from fear and fully conscious of spiritual invincibility. Jesus enjoyed the invigorating assurance of the possession of unflinching faith, and in each of life's trying situations he unfailingly exhibited an unquestioning loyalty to the Father's will. And this superb faith was undaunted even by the cruel and crushing threat of an ignominious death."

13 THE GIFT OF THE JESUS STORY

It is of record among those who were witness to the appearance of the Revelation, that a fourth set of papers appeared which contained an exhaustive account of the life and teachings of Jesus. This eight hundred-page narrative gives an almost day-by-day account of Jesus' life as he lived in and around Jerusalem during the times when Rome ruled its Empire, including Judea.

What makes this fourth section of the Revelation most intriguing is that it deviates from the format found within the first three sections of the papers in that a complete account of a person is retold from beginning to end. The first three sections of the papers were more or less elaborative answers to questions being asked by Sadler's group, whereas the Life and Teachings of Jesus were delivered as a completed series *all at once.* Part Four of the Revelation almost seems like a book unto itself, whereas parts one through three of the book are sequential in their dissemination; they are naturally and mutually dependent, continual and correlated explanations of the gradual levels of reality starting from the highest extending down to the lowest forms of existence.

The Jesus Papers' appearance suggests the Revelators decided to make yet a further revelation available so as to give us a full account of the last spiritually epochal event that occurred on our world. The Jesus Papers bring to full account, how the whole of spiritual existence and universal purpose culminates when its highest personality takes on the role of living life in human form on an evolutionary world; the Jesus Papers are complimentary to the life of the person whom the celestial authors call Christ Michael: The Creator Son who is the spiritual ruler of a segment of the universe whose worlds will eventually number ten million (of which we are a part). The Jesus Papers show the example and confirmation of what the eternal universe is really all about: the personal relationship between a spiritual creator and his spiritual children who inhabit the cosmos.

The breadth of knowledge contained in the Jesus Papers are not only exhaustive, they are also historically consistent. There have been studies made, for example, on the Jewish culture in the 1st Century. Historians have confirmed the village names, locations and the distances between various villages mentioned on the pages of the narrative. The Revelatory account of the social mores and cultural lifestyle of the average Jewish citizen of that era is *historically accurate.* Whoever wrote the Jesus papers would've had to be an expert historian and anthropologist. Scholars who have perused the revelatory material can attest to its historic accuracy.

There is also something else quite fascinating about the way the story is told. The authors had no trouble clarifying many supposed miracles that found their way into Christian theology. Authoritatively stated, the Jesus Papers are very clear about what were "miracles," and what were wholly natural events that took place during Jesus' 33 years of life.

The virgin birth evolved over time, a myth according to the Revelators, who state that virgin births have often been attributed to many spiritual leaders as a way of elevating their status to the miraculous, as is indicated with *Mithraism* (which early Christianity absorbed, as(we even celebrate Jesus's birthday on the same date of Mithras' birth on December 25th).

True, Joseph and Mary were selected as ideal parents capable of bringing up a child of promise, and Mary was visited by Gabriel prior to Jesus' birth, to allow her the emotional preparation when she was informed her child would be a 'child of promise,' but the Revelators are clear that Jesus was born naturally into the world, just as all babies are born - noting many references to the genetic strains of both Mary and Joseph that indicate the two were chosen in order to afford Jesus the best opportunity to inherit strong personality traits. While his birth may not have been of Immaculate Conception (getting pregnant without having sexual relations), it does not take away from the fact that a spiritual personality did incarnate in human form appearing as a babe in the manger. Mary and Joseph were chosen as the "ideal parents" to rear Jesus, but this was the only celestial circumstance or 'supernatural' connection relating to his birth, owing to the fact that celestial beings could trace the strong inheritance factors of both of Jesus' parents:

"Joseph, the human father of Jesus (Joshua ben Joseph), was a Hebrew of the Hebrews, albeit he carried many non-Jewish racial strains which had been added to his ancestral tree from time to time by the female lines of his progenitors. The ancestry of the father of Jesus went back to the days of Abraham and through this venerable patriarch to the earlier lines of inheritance leading to the Sumerians and Nodites and, through the southern tribes of the ancient blue man, to Andon and Fonta. David and Solomon were not in the direct line of Joseph's ancestry, neither did Joseph's lineage go directly back to Adam. Joseph's immediate ancestors were mechanics — builders, carpenters, masons, and smiths. Joseph himself was a carpenter and later a contractor. His family belonged to a long and illustrious line of the nobility of the common people, accentuated ever and anon by the appearance of unusual individuals who had distinguished themselves in connection with the evolution of religion on Urantia.

Mary, the earth mother of Jesus, was a descendant of a long line of unique ancestors embracing many of the most remarkable women in the racial history of Urantia. Although Mary was an average woman of her day and generation, possessing a fairly normal temperament, she reckoned among her ancestors such well-known women as Annon, Tamar, Ruth, Bathsheba, Ansie, Cloa, Eve, Enta, and Ratta. No Jewish woman of that day had a more illustrious lineage of common progenitors or one extending back to more auspicious beginnings. Mary's ancestry, like Joseph's, was characterized by the predominance of strong but average individuals, relieved now and then by numerous outstanding personalities in the march of civilization and the progressive evolution of religion. Racially considered, it is hardly proper to regard Mary as a Jewess. In culture and belief she was a Jew, but in hereditary endowment she was more a composite of Syrian, Hittite, Phoenician, Greek, and Egyptian stocks, her racial inheritance being more general than that of Joseph.

Of all couples living in Palestine at about the time of Michael's projected bestowal, Joseph and Mary possessed the most ideal combination of widespread racial connections and superior average of personality endowments. It was the plan of Michael to appear on earth as an average man, that the common people might understand him and receive him; wherefore Gabriel selected just such persons as Joseph and Mary to become the bestowal parents." (Paper 121, Section 1, Para. 1)

On Jesus and what Joseph and Mary contributed to his character, the Revelators write:

"Jesus derived much of his unusual gentleness and marvelous sympathetic understanding of human nature from his father; he inherited his gift as a great teacher and his tremendous capacity for righteous indignation from his mother. In emotional reactions to his adult-life environment, Jesus was at one time like his father, meditative and worshipful, sometimes characterized by apparent sadness; but more often he drove forward in the manner of his mother's optimistic and determined disposition. All in all, Mary's temperament tended to dominate the career of the divine Son as he grew up and swung into the momentous strides of his adult life. In some particulars Jesus was a blending of his parents' traits; in other respects he exhibited the traits of one in contrast with those of the other."

True that Jesus chose earth as the world of his bestowal, and the reasons are stated that the time and place of Jesus birth had more to do with Jerusalem being a literal *crossroads* of the then civilized world, such a circumstance which would allow the quick dissemination of his gospel:

"In the centuries just prior to these times Greek culture and the Greek language had spread over Occident and near Orient, and the Jews, being a Levantine race, in nature part Occidental and part Oriental, were eminently fitted to utilize such cultural and linguistic settings for the effective spread of a new religion to both East and West. These most favorable circumstances were further enhanced by the tolerant political rule of the Mediterranean world by the Romans."

It is stated very clearly that Jesus was a *new revelation of truth to mankind,* that his life and the way he lived it was the true miracle, not the walking on water, the catching of fish, or even the healing of the many sick that "touched his garment."

While the papers specifically uncover many so-called miracles which were in fact, wholly natural events, they also more fully explained how, on some specific occasions, actual "miracles" did occur and did transpire because of Jesus' divine attributes *in accordance with the will of his Heavenly Father.*

Take for example, the changing of wine into water:

"The father of the bridegroom had provided plenty of wine for all the guests bidden to the marriage feast, but how was he to know that the marriage of his son was to become an event so closely associated with the expected manifestation of Jesus as the Messianic deliverer? He was delighted to have the honor of numbering the celebrated Galilean among his guests, but before the wedding supper was over, the servants brought him the disconcerting news that the wine was running short. By the time the formal supper had ended and the guests were strolling about in the garden, the mother of the bridegroom confided to Mary that the supply of wine was exhausted. And Mary confidently said: "Have no worry — I will speak to my son. He will help us." And thus did she presume to speak, notwithstanding the rebuke of but a few hours before.

Throughout a period of many years, Mary had always turned to Jesus for help in every crisis of their home life at Nazareth so that it was only natural for her to think of him at this time. But this ambitious mother had still other motives for appealing to her eldest son on this occasion. As Jesus was standing alone in a corner of the garden, his mother approached him, saying, "My son, they have no wine." And Jesus answered, "My good woman, what have I to do with that?" Said Mary, "But I believe your hour has come; cannot you help us?" Jesus replied: "Again I declare that I have not come to do things in this wise. Why do you trouble me again with these matters?" And then, breaking down in tears, Mary entreated him, "But, my son, I promised them that you would help us; won't you please do something for me?" And then spoke Jesus: "Woman, what have you to do with making such promises? See that you do it not again. We must in all things wait upon the will of the Father in heaven."

Mary the mother of Jesus was crushed; she was stunned! As she stood there before him motionless, with the tears streaming down her face, the human heart of Jesus was overcome with compassion for the woman who had borne him in the flesh; and bending forward, he laid his hand tenderly upon her head, saying: "Now, now, Mother Mary, grieve not over my apparently hard sayings, for have I not many times told you that I have come only to do the will of my heavenly Father? Most gladly would I do what you ask of me if it were a part of the Father's will — "and Jesus stopped short, he hesitated. Mary seemed to sense that something was happening. Leaping up, she threw her arms around Jesus' neck, kissed him, and rushed off to the servants' quarters, saying, "Whatever my son says, that do." But Jesus said nothing. He now realized that he had already said — or rather desirefully thought — too much.

Mary was dancing with glee. She did not know how the wine would be produced, but she confidently believed that she had finally persuaded her first-born son to assert his authority, to dare to step forth and claim his position and exhibit his Messianic power. And, because of the presence and association of certain universe powers and personalities, of which all those present were *wholly ignorant, she was not to be disappointed. The wine Mary desired and which Jesus, the God-man, humanly and sympathetically wished for, was forthcoming.*

Near at hand stood six water pots of stone, filled with water, holding about twenty gallons apiece. This water was intended for subsequent use in the final purification ceremonies of the wedding celebration. The commotion of the servants about these huge stone vessels, under the busy direction of his mother, attracted Jesus' attention, and going over, he observed that they were drawing wine out of them by the pitcherful.

It was gradually dawning upon Jesus what had happened. Of all persons present at the marriage feast of Cana, Jesus was the most surprised. Others had expected him to work a wonder, but that was just what he had purposed not to do. And then the Son of Man recalled the admonition of his Personalized Thought Adjuster (Spirit of the Father) in the hills. He recounted how the Adjuster had warned him about the inability of any power or personality to deprive him of the creator prerogative of independence of time. On this occasion power transformers, midwayers, and all other required personalities were assembled near the water and other necessary elements, and in the face of the expressed wish of the Universe Creator Sovereign, there was no escaping the instantaneous appearance of wine. And this occurrence was made doubly certain since the Personalized Adjuster had signified that the execution of the Son's desire was in no way a contravention of the Father's will. " (Paper 137, Section 4)

For those who claim to love Jesus, the Urantia Book allows such lovers of Christ to fully immerse themselves into the life and *living* of their Savior.

Chronologically, the papers follow the lad through his later teen and early adult years, his experiences as a traveler throughout the Mediterranean, his contacts with the Greeks, the Romans, and other cultures during his many visits to Jerusalem, Alexandria and other cities throughout the Roman Empire. The stories include how Jesus absorbed and embraced man's culture in order to understand men, how he transformed the lives of those he met and planted the seeds of truth during his travels, so that his later disciples would find easier receptivity to this "Scribe of Damascus," who had initially introduced truth to the people he met *prior* to his public ministry.

Narratives tell the story of Jesus and his days training and living with his Apostles, his rigorous instruction to them and to the multitudes who were hearing a new saving message that "set men free" from the bonds of a merciless and enslaving religion.

Further reading of the Jesus Papers disclose his final years on earth, how the religious rulers of his day feared him and his bold new teachings, how Jesus himself was deeply saddened over the realization that his own life would ultimately end with overwhelming rejection from even his people:

"And now, as I am about to leave you, I would speak words of comfort. Peace I leave with you; my peace I give to you. I make these gifts not as the world gives--by measure--I give each of you all you will receive. Let not your heart be troubled, neither let it be fearful. I have overcome the world, and in me you shall all triumph through faith. I have warned you that the Son of Man will be killed, but I assure you I will come back before I go to the Father, even though it be for only a little while. And after I have ascended to the Father, I will surely send the new teacher to be with you and to abide in your very hearts. And when you see all this come to pass, be not dismayed, but rather believe, inasmuch as you knew it all beforehand. I have loved you with a great affection, and I would not leave you, but it is the Father's will. My hour has come."

The Revelators indicate on more than one occasion that this account has the potential to bring about a worldwide renaissance as to the real nature of Jesus and why he lived among us:

"The world needs more firsthand religion. Even Christianity — the best of the religions of the twentieth century — is not only a religion about Jesus, but it is so largely one which men experience secondhand. They take their religion wholly as handed down by

their accepted religious teachers. What an awakening the world would experience if it could only see Jesus as he really lived on earth and know, firsthand, his life-giving teachings! Descriptive words of things beautiful cannot thrill like the sight thereof; neither can creedal words inspire men's souls like the experience of knowing the presence of God. But expectant faith will ever keep the hope-door of man's soul open for the entrance of the eternal spiritual realities of the divine values of the worlds beyond." (Paper 195, Section 9, Para. 3)

"Christianity has indeed done a great service for this world, but what is now most needed is Jesus. The world needs to see Jesus living again on earth in the experience of spirit-born mortals who effectively reveal the Master to all men. It is futile to talk about a revival of primitive Christianity; you must go forward from where you find yourselves. Modern culture must become spiritually baptized with a new revelation of Jesus' life and illuminated with a new understanding of his gospel of eternal salvation. And when Jesus becomes thus lifted up, he will draw all men to himself. Jesus' disciples should be more than conquerors, even overflowing sources of inspiration and enhanced living to all men. Religion is only an exalted humanism until it is made divine by the discovery of the reality of the presence of God in personal experience." (Paper 195, Section 10, Para. 1)

14 THE DANGERS OF SECULARISM

It is impossible to understand modern day secularism without giving some consideration to the way in which revealed religion has had its message carried on down through the ages, and how this same revealed religion has been distorted and twisted as it was disseminated by the many cultures who have come into contact with those truths, and especially how secularism evolved *as a protest* to the misuse by those religions inspired by revelation. Secularism today is a protest against the laws of an institutional and overly dogmatized religion:

"At the time of this revelation, the prevailing intellectual and philosophical climate of both European and American life is decidedly secular—humanistic. For three hundred years Western thinking has been progressively secularized. Religion has become more and more a nominal influence, largely a ritualistic exercise. The majority of professed Christians of Western civilization are unwittingly actual secularists.

It required a great power, a mighty influence, to free the thinking and living of the Western peoples from the withering grasp of a totalitarian ecclesiastical domination. Secularism did break the bonds of church control, and now in turn it threatens to establish a new and godless type of mastery over the hearts and minds of modern man. The tyrannical and dictatorial political state is the direct offspring of scientific materialism and philosophic secularism. Secularism no sooner frees man from the domination of the institutionalized church than it sells him into slavish bondage to the totalitarian state. Secularism frees man from ecclesiastical slavery only to betray him into the tyranny of political and economic slavery."

"To the secularistic revolt you owe the amazing creativity of American industrialism and the unprecedented material progress of Western civilization. And because the secularistic revolt went too far and lost sight of God and true religion, there also followed the unlooked-for harvest of world wars and international unsettledness.

It is not necessary to sacrifice faith in God in order to enjoy the blessings of the modern secularistic revolt: tolerance, social service, democratic government, and civil liberties. It was not necessary for the secularists to antagonize true religion in order to promote science and to advance education.

But secularism is not the sole parent of all these recent gains in the enlargement of living. Behind the gains of the twentieth century are not only science and secularism but also the unrecognized and unacknowledged spiritual workings of the life and teaching of Jesus of Nazareth.

Without God, without religion, scientific secularism can never co-ordinate its forces, harmonize its divergent and rivalrous interests, races, and nationalisms. This secularistic human society, notwithstanding its unparalleled materialistic achievement, is slowly disintegrating. The chief cohesive force resisting this disintegration of antagonism is nationalism. And nationalism is the chief barrier to world peace.

The inherent weakness of secularism is that it discards ethics and religion for politics and power. You simply cannot establish the brotherhood of men while ignoring or denying the fatherhood of God.

Secular social and political optimism is an illusion. Without God, neither freedom and liberty, nor property and wealth will lead to peace." (Paper 195, Section 8)

Even if secularism were to completely rule the day, it would still not extinguish man's deep-seated religious impulse. Man will always yearn for understanding of that he cannot explain.

Religion will always be a part of his nature but from the societal standpoint, as long as religion imposes authority over him, man will distrust institutional religious authority.

The appeal of secularism is that it affords man a sense of peace in that he no longer questions his purpose of destiny from a supposed spiritual point of view. Ignorance of that which he cannot know does bring a sort of peace. The problem with secularism on a group level is that remains superficial. Morality also becomes relative in the world of the secularist. Man becomes the final authority, which has often led to totalitarianism regimes. For the same reasons man is driven away from the overbearing laws of the church is man driven right back into the arms of an authoritative regime based on godless or humanist doctrine – ultimate power given to men over men.

The Revelators say secularism cannot bring universal peace to mankind because its foundation is only temporal; the only potent force capable of bringing man to a worldwide recognition of brotherhood is a divine and loving Creator. Brotherly love can only be achieved by the recognition of a supreme "Father."

The goal of the ages, for mortal evolutionary man, is the spiritual attainment of peace and prosperity through mutual love and trust for one another. Secularism might bring man temporary or superficial peace, but it offers no spiritual motivation for keeping the peace. Unless man sees himself as being part of a larger, spiritual family, the goal of peace will not endure on the foundation based a secularist philospohy:

"Materialism denies God, secularism simply ignores him; at least that was the earlier attitude. More recently, secularism has assumed a more militant attitude, assuming to take the place of the religion whose totalitarian bondage it onetime resisted. Twentieth-century secularism tends to affirm that man does not need God. But beware! this godless philosophy of human society will lead only to unrest, animosity, unhappiness, war, and world-wide disaster." (Paper 195, Section 8, Para. 5)

Secularism may indeed be a Trojan horse to a later appearance of a spiritual renaissance. After all, since secularism was a reaction to authority; it freed man from the bondage of those religious institutions who maintained control over them, but now free, it is hoped thinking men will give time to reflect on true spiritual values.

As a whole, society can be viewed as grasping for philosophical meaning. The popularity of religion is proof that secularism is not the end all solution to a happy and fulfilling life. Those who choose secularism as a philosophy of life may find it easier to live in a complex social order which constantly beckons us to "feed the machine," which is materialism.

The great challenge of the modern age will be for man to find a religion that doesn't conflict with science and has philosophic meaning. In other words, man must find the God of the 21st century, a God that is both personal, and inspiring, but not one who requires of man that he forsake intellectual integrity in order to be allowed entrance into this 'kingdom.' The thinking man of this new era must find God in his own way:

"The modern age will refuse to accept a religion which is inconsistent with facts and out of harmony with its highest conceptions of truth, beauty, and goodness. The hour is striking for a rediscovery of the true and original foundations of present-day distorted and compromised Christianity—the real life and teachings of Jesus. "Primitive man lived a life of superstitious bondage to religious fear. Modern, civilized men dread the thought of falling under the dominance of strong religious convictions.

Thinking man has always feared to be held by a religion. When a strong and moving religion threatens to dominate him, he invariably tries to rationalize, traditionalize, and institutionalize it, thereby hoping to gain control of it. By such procedure, even a revealed religion becomes man-made and man-dominated. Modern men and women of intelligence evade the religion of Jesus because of their fears of what it will do to them—and with them. And all such fears are well founded. The religion of Jesus does, indeed, dominate and transform its believers, demanding that men dedicate their lives to seeking for a knowledge of the will of the Father in heaven and requiring that the energies of living be consecrated to the unselfish service of the brotherhood of man" *(Paper 195, Section 9, Para. 5, 6)*

It is for this reason alone I believe the Revelators desired to present enlarged concepts of truth and cosmic understanding that, while these might be strikingly different from what we are told by our bible or church, are at least more consistent with the thoughts and perceptions of the 21st century.

The Revelators have in effect, updated religion by providing enlarged concepts that previous generations could not have accepted. You can say the new message of the Urantia Book might have come at a time when modern man was intellectually able to understand it.

15 THE PRESENT AND FUTURE STATE OF MAN

The shelves of any bookstore are lined with everyone's published opinion of what the future holds for mankind. We all are unsure of our future; we cling to the hope that we will, as a species, survive what lies ahead. Yet solutions are scarce on just how we will solve the world's problems of mass starvation, overpopulation, political conflict, etc.

Recent polls suggest most adults cite economic and environmental issues as the primary cause of concern. Thirty percent of the American adult population uses some form of anti-depressant to help cope with the anxiety that is called modern day.

Man literally stands at an apex of either social collapse or the dawning of a new age. And it doesn't take but a few moments glance at the evening news to sense man faces grave danger at every perceivable turn.

The Revelators make it very clear that man is approaching an ideological struggle he has never faced before. It is commonly believed (though the authors never make the claim) that perhaps the reason the revelation appeared in this age is exactly because of the apex humanity has reached. The evolutionary wheels of progress have culminated to a point where mankind has to deal with social and ethical problems never before faced. We have made great progress, the Revelators write in 1935, but we have also come to a moral and ethical standstill:

"The greatest twentieth-century influences contributing to the furtherance of civilization and the advancement of culture are the marked increase in world travel and the unparalleled improvements in methods of communication. But the improvement in education has not kept pace with the expanding social structure; neither has the modern appreciation of ethics developed in correspondence with growth along more purely intellectual and scientific lines. And modern civilization is at a standstill in spiritual development and the safeguarding of the home institution."

Computers revolutionized the way we work and to a large degree the way we think. We embraced it and there is no turning back. The Internet connected us, eliminated borders and continents by allowing all of us to exchange, access and store information. Satellites and digital broadcasting allows us to see and hear virtually anyone, anywhere. As the microprocessor gets smaller, people become more connected in ways even our parents could never have dreamed.

Technology proves how far we have come, of how much potential we have, and even if we sometimes abuse and use it for the wrong reasons, the technology we have access to has already begun to transform the entire world. The idea of distributing news around the world in seconds is a remarkable achievement; it has brought us closer, and has made us more aware of not just our neighbors next door or down the street, but of our neighbors across the country and around the world.

It cannot be understated - nor can it be forgotten - that mankind crossed a major threshold when the computer age arrived, when the first email was sent and received. Universal brotherhood has never been easier to attain because of this connectivity. We are, contrary to impressions you receive from the news headlines, one step closer to peace on Earth, 'goodwill among men' because this technology has made it more feasible to attain than ever before. Technology allows us to share everything. Potential greatness in human understanding and a real building of a cooperative spirit among men is now attainable through and because of the digital age, 'The Information Age.'

The Revelators state the course on most evolutionary worlds is towards universal brotherhood, peace and goodwill among men, for this is the ultimate goal of pursuit. How long it takes depends very much on several factors, including language, economical factors, cultural literacy, and religious tolerance. The Revelators remain optimistic of our potential of achieving worldwide peace, as the foundation for such peace has already been laid.

In the following excerpt from Paper 52 entitled *Planetary Mortal Epochs*, the author's outline the challenges we face, owing to our extraordinary planetary history:

"The bestowal Son is the Prince of Peace. He arrives with the message, "Peace on earth and good will among men."

On normal worlds this is a dispensation of world-wide peace; the nations no more learn war. But such salutary influences did not attend the coming of your bestowal Son, Christ Michael. Urantia is not proceeding in the normal order. Your world is out of step in the planetary procession. Your Master, when on earth, warned his disciples that his advent would not bring the usual reign of peace on Urantia. He distinctly told them that there would be "wars and rumors of wars," and that nation would rise against nation. At another time he said, "Think not that I have come to bring peace upon earth."

Even on normal evolutionary worlds the realization of the world-wide brotherhood of man is not an easy accomplishment. On a confused and disordered planet like Urantia such an achievement requires a much longer time and necessitates far greater effort. Unaided social evolution can hardly achieve such happy results on a spiritually isolated sphere. Religious revelation is essential to the realization of brotherhood on Urantia. While Jesus has shown the way to the immediate attainment of spiritual brotherhood, the realization of social brotherhood on your world depends much on the achievement of the following personal transformations and planetary adjustments:

*1. **Social fraternity.** Multiplication of international and interracial social contacts and fraternal associations through* *travel, commerce, and competitive play. Development of a common language and the multiplication of multilinguists. The racial and national interchange of students, teachers, industrialists, and religious philosophers.*

*2. **Intellectual cross-fertilization.** Brotherhood is impossible on a world whose inhabitants are so primitive that they fail to recognize the folly of unmitigated selfishness. There must occur an exchange of national and racial literature. Each race must become familiar with the thought of all races; each nation must know the feelings of all nations. Ignorance breeds suspicion, and suspicion is incompatible with the essential attitude of sympathy and love.*

*3. **Ethical awakening.** Only ethical consciousness can unmask the immorality of human intolerance and the sinfulness of fratricidal strife. Only a moral conscience can condemn the evils of national envy and racial jealousy. Only moral beings will ever seek for that spiritual insight which is essential to living the golden rule.*

*4. **Political wisdom.** Emotional maturity is essential to self-control. Only emotional maturity will insure the substitution of international techniques of civilized adjudication for the barbarous arbitrament of war. Wise statesmen will sometime work for the welfare of humanity even while they strive to promote the interest of their national or racial groups. Selfish political sagacity is ultimately suicidal — destructive of all those enduring qualities which insure planetary group survival.*

*5. **Spiritual insight.** The brotherhood of man is, after all, predicated on the recognition of the fatherhood of God. The quickest way to realize the brotherhood of man on Urantia is to effect the spiritual transformation of present-day humanity. The only technique for accelerating the natural trend of social evolution is that of applying spiritual pressure from above, thus augmenting moral insight while enhancing the soul capacity of every mortal to understand and love every other mortal. Mutual understanding and fraternal love are transcendent civilizers and mighty factors in the world-wide realization of the brotherhood of man." (Paper 52, Section 6)*

We appear to be at about step two, but just barely. Travel, communications and technology have brought us closer together, but the need for a *real ethical awakening*, for true political wisdom on the part of our world leaders through true spiritual enlightenment on a worldwide level should help us progress quickly.

Much of the international peace we have today is due to our interconnectivity and our mutual dependence through trade, commerce and language. While some countries still battle one another over natural and economic resources, yet, the more progressive nations accepted our mutual interdependence of one another.

For example, China and America are ideologically very different, yet economically we are linked. Not long ago we were ready to exchange nuclear warheads, now we exchange business cards and economic advisors.

Within a relatively short time span, English has become the assumed (if not the official) universal language; pilots use it to navigate; most other nations teach it as a primary or mandated secondary language. Indeed, communication of ideas between nations has never been better because of the widespread use of one major language. The use of one common language is an incredible step towards world peace in that it allows billions of people to communicate freely. This step in global communication is unprecedented.

The Revelators also know that while our technology and scientific progress would achieve new heights, materialism or a lack of true spiritual growth will present its own set of problems:

"At the time of this writing the worst of the materialistic age is over; the day of a better understanding is already beginning to dawn. The higher minds of the scientific world are no longer wholly materialistic in their philosophy, but the rank and file of the people still lean in that direction as a result of former teachings. But this age of physical realism is only a passing episode in man's life on earth. Modern science has left true religion--the teachings of Jesus as translated in the lives of his believers--untouched. All

science has done is to destroy the childlike illusions of the misinterpretations of life."

The next step for modern man, according the Urantia Book, is for him to address his religious and spiritual understanding. A strong foundation for any civilized society must be based on spiritual principles, not material ones:

"The violent swing from an age of miracles to an age of machines has proved altogether upsetting to man. The cleverness and dexterity of the false philosophies of mechanism belie their very mechanistic contentions. The fatalistic agility of the mind of a materialist forever disproves his assertions that the universe is a blind and purposeless energy phenomenon.

The mechanistic naturalism of some supposedly educated men and the thoughtless secularism of the man in the street are both exclusively concerned with things; they are barren of all real values, sanctions, and satisfactions of a spiritual nature, as well as being devoid of faith, hope, and eternal assurances. One of the great troubles with modern life is that man thinks he is too busy to find time for spiritual meditation and religious devotion.

Materialism reduces man to a soulless automaton and constitutes him merely an arithmetical symbol finding a helpless place in the mathematical formula of an unromantic and mechanistic universe. But whence comes all this vast universe of mathematics without a Master Mathematician? Science may expatiate on the conservation of matter, but religion validates the conservation of men's souls--it concerns their experience with spiritual realities and eternal values."

The great challenge for us at this time is to search for real meaning and truth, to contemplate the higher realities of our existence and not just the day-to-day affairs of existence.

Materialism and secularism pose a real threat, according to the Revelators:

"The inherent weakness of secularism is that it discards ethics and religion for politics and power. You simply cannot establish

the brotherhood of men while ignoring or denying the fatherhood of God."

"Secular social and political optimism is an illusion. Without God, neither freedom and liberty, nor property and wealth will lead to peace."

"The complete secularization of science, education, industry, and society can lead only to disaster. During the first third of the twentieth century Urantians killed more human beings than were killed during the whole of the Christian dispensation up to that time. And this is only the beginning of the dire harvest of materialism and secularism; still more terrible destruction is yet to come."

Remembering that the Urantia Book was written in 1934, so the final sentence of the paragraph *'more terrible destruction is yet to come'* bespeaks a prophetic tone as World War II erupted just five years later.

Technology has brought us closer together and better technology will no doubt push us along the evolutionary path of progress, but what role does religion have in a progressive society?

The modern dilemma for all of us seems to be whether there can be a spiritual balance that tempers the materialistic urge to consume physical pleasures at the risk of becoming essentially what amounts to be a godless society.

What the world needs now, so say the Revelators, is a new presentation of Jesus' teachings:

"Selfish men and women simply will not pay such a price for even the greatest spiritual treasure ever offered mortal man. Only when man has become sufficiently disillusioned by the sorrowful disappointments attendant upon the foolish and deceptive pursuits of selfishness, and subsequent to the discovery of the barrenness of formalized religion, will he be disposed to turn wholeheartedly to the gospel of the kingdom, the religion of Jesus of Nazareth."

The world needs more firsthand religion. Even Christianity-- the best of the religions of the twentieth century--is not only a religion about Jesus, but it is so largely one which men experience secondhand. They take their religion wholly as handed down by their accepted religious teachers. What an awakening the world would experience if it could only see Jesus as he really lived on earth and know, firsthand, his life-giving teachings!

Descriptive words of things beautiful cannot thrill like the sight thereof; neither can creedal words inspire men's souls like the experience of knowing the presence of God. But expectant faith will ever keep the hope-door of man's soul open for the entrance of the eternal spiritual realities of the divine values of the worlds beyond."

The Urantia Book presents to us the *Life and Teachings of Jesus*. While the first three parts of the book reveal and calibrate historical knowledge (our origins), the final series of papers containing the life and teachings of Jesus, were meant for us to learn again – firsthand – the religion *of* Jesus.

If just three years of Jesus life in Scripture can change the world as much as it has over the past two-thousand years, imagine what his entire life's teachings could do to inspire human brotherhood?

If one accepts the premise that whoever authored the Urantia Book had factual knowledge, as we have explored thus far, then pause to consider that - *for the first time* - an exhaustive narrative of the man who changed religion (and to a certain extent, Western Civilization) now exists for every to experience *firsthand*.

The real religion of Jesus will eventually triumph:

"The kingdom of God is within you" was probably the greatest pronouncement Jesus ever made, next to the declaration that his Father is a living and loving spirit.

In winning souls for the Master, it is not the first mile of compulsion, duty, or convention that will transform man and his world, but rather the second mile of free service and liberty-loving devotion that betokens the Jesusonian reaching forth to grasp his brother in love and sweep him on under spiritual guidance toward the higher and divine goal of mortal existence. Christianity even now willingly goes the first mile, but mankind languishes and stumbles along in moral darkness because there are so few genuine second-milers--so few professed followers of Jesus who really live and love as he taught his disciples to live and love and serve."

The call to the adventure of building a new and transformed human society by means of the spiritual rebirth of Jesus' brotherhood of the kingdom should thrill all who believe in him as men have not been stirred since the days when they walked about on earth as his companions in the flesh."

Religion, if it is to serve its better purpose, must cease being apolitical or social lever, and transform itself in an inspirational mechanism for social change:

The hope of modern Christianity is that it should cease to sponsor the social systems and industrial policies of Western civilization while it humbly bows itself before the cross it so valiantly extols, there to learn anew from Jesus of Nazareth the greatest truths mortal man can ever hear--the living gospel of the fatherhood of God and the brotherhood of man."

The fact that all people from every corner of the earth can in some form or another, communicate with one another incredible as well as unprecedented. The quality of that relationship is dependent on how we view ourselves in the grand scheme of things. If the plan is for worldwide peace, if our destiny is spiritual and not just for material consumption, then we must view the glass half full.

The Urantia Book provides optimism because it lifts the curtain back on the real purpose of our struggles, and it provides us a vision of how we can achieve this supernal goal of the ages:

"Man's forward spiritual urge is not a psychic illusion. All of man's universe romancing may not be fact, but much, very much, is truth.

Some men's lives are too great and noble to descend to the low level of being merely successful. The animal must adapt itself to the environment, but the religious man transcends his environment and in this way escapes the limitations of the present material world through this insight of divine love. This concept of love generates in the soul of man that super animal effort to find truth, beauty, and goodness; and when he does find them, he is glorified in their embrace; he is consumed with the desire to live them, to do righteousness."

Be not discouraged; human evolution is still in progress, and the revelation of God to the world, in and through Jesus, shall not fail."

To those who may think that the Urantia Book is some offshoot of a Christian religion, it is not. The Jesus of the accepted Christian faith and the Jesus in the Urantia Book are indeed one in the same person, but the religion *of* Jesus, as opposed to a religion *about* Jesus offers two very different interpretations, and honest seekers of truth should be willing examine Jesus' life more fully, for there is much, much more to the story.

The following passage states the hopes of the authors' desire for humanity to rediscover the Master's teachings:

"The time is ripe to witness the figurative resurrection of the human Jesus from his burial tomb amidst the theological traditions and the religious dogmas of nineteen centuries. Jesus of Nazareth must not be longer sacrificed to even the splendid concept of the glorified Christ. What a transcendent service if, through this revelation, the Son of Man should be recovered from the tomb of traditional theology and be presented as the living Jesus to the church that bears his name, and to all other religions! Surely the Christian fellowship of believers will not hesitate to make such adjustments of faith and of practices of living as will enable it to "follow after" the Master in the demonstration of his real life of religious devotion to the doing of his Father's will and of consecration to the unselfish service of man. Do professed Christians fear the exposure of a self-sufficient and unconsecrated fellowship of social respectability and selfish economic maladjustment? Does institutional Christianity fear the possible jeopardy, or even the overthrow, of traditional ecclesiastical authority if the Jesus of Galilee is reinstated in the minds and souls

of mortal men as the ideal of personal religious living? Indeed, the social readjustments, the economic transformations, the moral rejuvenations, and the religious revisions of Christian civilization would be drastic and revolutionary if the living religion of Jesus should suddenly supplant the theological religion about Jesus."

16 THE SPIRIT IN MAN

The Urantia Papers explore the reality of *spirit within man*.

It is disclosed that every person, after the age of about five becomes endowed with a fragment of the Father's spirit (called a *Thought Adjuster* or *Mystery Monitor*).

It is explained that at about the time a child makes his first moral choice, a living spirit become identified with, and continues to be a part of, that person throughout his existence. To a greater or lesser degree, a person is obedient to its leadings, or he is not. This spirit comes from the Divine Creator, says the Revelation, all spiritual beings are drawn to their spiritual source.

It is this same fragment of spirit that identifies us as being more than mere material, or animal. Every religion has a name for it. We all know what it is. Some call it the Holy Spirit, others call it the Holy Ghost, some call it the ka, and still others recognize it as the spark of life or the Fathers' *anointed spirit*.

The Revelators go to great lengths to make sure we understand it is *real* and it is the single most important spiritual influence we have in our mortal existence.

The spirit of God is our only link that bridges the infinite gap between man and his spiritual Father. After it enters us, it remains with us, ever leading us to higher impulses of true insightful thought; it beckons us to cooperate with its leadings and it comforts us when we are in our darkest hour.

Sadly, the Revelators say many are either too afraid, or too egotistical to embrace it for fear we might be wrong. Besides the reality of God, the papers emphasize this fragment living within each human being as the single most influence in our lives:

"The mortals of the realms of time and space may differ greatly in innate abilities and intellectual endowment, they may enjoy environments exceptionally favorable to social advancement and moral progress, or they may suffer from the lack of almost every human aid to culture and supposed advancement in the arts of civilization; but the possibilities for spiritual progress in the ascension career are equal to all; increasing levels of spiritual insight and cosmic meanings are attained quite independently of all such socio-moral differentials of the diversified material environments on the evolutionary worlds."

"However mortal man may differ in their intellectual, social, economic, and even moral opportunities and endowments, forget not that their spiritual endowment is uniform and unique. They all enjoy the same divine presence of the gift from the Father, and they are all equally privileged to seek intimate personal communion with this indwelling spirit of divine origin, while they may all equally choose to accept the uniform spiritual leading of these Mystery Monitors."

"If mortal man is wholeheartedly spiritually motivated, unreservedly consecrated to the doing of the Father's will, then, since he is so certainly and so effectively spiritually endowed by the indwelling and divine Adjuster (spirit of God), there cannot fail to materialize in that individual's experience the sublime consciousness of knowing God and the supernal assurance of surviving for the purpose of finding God by the progressive experience of becoming more and more like him." (Paper 5, Section 1, 2, 3)

The greatest articulation on the *spirit in man* and the arena of how the physical and spiritual natures are played out in mortal life comes from an astounding confession made by a Seraphic Guardian of Destiny, in giving testimony to her

146

superiors on challenges she observed while giving assistance to her mortal subject:

"Much of my difficulty was due to the unending conflict between the two natures of my subject: the urge of ambition opposed by animal indolence; the ideals of a superior people crossed by the instincts of an inferior race; the high purposes of a great mind antagonized by the urge of a primitive inheritance; the long-distance view of a far-seeing Monitor (God's eternal spirit) counteracted by the nearsightedness of a creature of time; the progressive plans of an ascending being modified by the desires and longings of a material nature; the flashes of universe intelligence cancelled by the chemical-energy mandates of the evolving race; the urge of angels opposed by the emotions of an animal; the training of an intellect annulled by the tendencies of instinct; the experience of the individual opposed by the accumulated propensities of the race; the aims of the best overshadowed by the drift of the worst; the flight of genius neutralized by the gravity of mediocrity; the progress of the good retarded by the inertia of the bad; the art of the beautiful besmirched by the presence of evil; the buoyancy of health neutralized by the debility of disease; the fountain of faith polluted by the poisons of fear; the spring of joy embittered by the waters of sorrow; the gladness of anticipation disillusioned by the bitterness of realization; the joys of living ever threatened by the sorrows of death. Such a life on such a planet! And yet, because of the ever-present help and urge of the Thought Adjuster (Gods' Spirit), this soul did achieve a fair degree of happiness and success and has even now ascended to the judgment halls of mansonia." (Paper 111, Section 7, Para. 6)

Perhaps in this confession, we can begin to understand why the conflicts we face in this mortal existence are so challenging, so daunting. Is there anyone reading these words who doesn't have firsthand experience in the pull between our animal natures and our spiritual impulses, our desire to do good against the backdrop of the world where we must also fight for survival?

Man's animal and spiritual natures are in constant battle, but the spiritual nature *will triumph*:

"The doing of the will of God is nothing more or less than an exhibition of creature willingness to share the inner life with God — with the very God who has made such a creature life of inner meaning-value possible. Sharing is Godlike — divine. God shares all with the Eternal Son and the Infinite Spirit, while they, in turn, share all things with the divine Sons and spirit Daughters of the universes.

The imitation of God is the key to perfection; the doing of his will is the secret of survival and of perfection in survival.

Mortals live in God, and so God has willed to live in mortals. As men trust themselves to him, so has he — and first — trusted a part of himself to be with men; has consented to live in men and to indwell men subject to the human will.

Peace in this life, survival in death, perfection in the next life, service in eternity — all these are achieved (in spirit) now when the creature personality consents — chooses — to subject the creature will to the Father's will. And already has the Father chosen to make a fragment of himself subject to the will of the creature personality.

Such a creature choice is not a surrender of will. It is a consecration of will, an expansion of will, a glorification of will, a perfecting of will; and such choosing raises the creature will from the level of temporal significance to that higher estate wherein the personality of the creature son communes with the personality of the spirit Father.

This choosing of the Father's will is the spiritual finding of the spirit Father by mortal man, even though an age must pass before the creature son may actually stand in the factual presence of God on Paradise. This choosing does not so much consist in the negation of creature will — "Not my will but yours be done" — as it consists in the creature's positive affirmation: "It is my will that your will be done." And if this choice is made, sooner or later will the God-choosing son find inner union (fusion) with the indwelling God fragment, while this same perfecting son will find supreme personality satisfaction in the worship communion of the personality of man and the personality of his Maker, two personalities whose creative attributes have eternally joined in self-willed mutuality of expression — the birth of another eternal partnership of the will of man and the will of God." (Paper 111, Section 5)

We are not watched--*we are cared for*. We are not played with or manipulated--we are tested and challenged to be better. The struggles of daily living are methods used to strengthen our character.

If we begin to see ourselves as being part of a larger circle of existence, or if man can enlarge his place and purpose in the cosmos, then life becomes *an exalted privilege*.

Man being the end result of an accidental universe demands nothing of him. An existence in a living universe intelligently and purposively controlled demands of man a cooperative effort towards perfection.

If what the book says is true about millions of inhabited worlds being literal spawning grounds for evolutionary life, and if these same worlds are under the guidance and supervision of angels, counselors and other unseen spiritual forces, and if there is a mandate hailing from the Creator declaring "Be you perfect, even as I am perfect," with all of everything striving in a cooperative effort for perfection, then doesn't this portrayal of reality provide much greater motivation for living life well, as opposed to the limited viewpoint of seeing ourselves as isolated mortals living on a lonely blue planet spinning forever in space without a clear and distinctive purpose?

And if it is true we are just accidents of space, a cause and effect result of natural biological eventuation, without ultimate or infinite purpose, if this is the fact of existence, the true reality, then why do we strive for something different? Why does man hope? Why does man dare to think otherwise?

The Revelators say man clings to these hopes because he is *instilled with a spiritual force* that drives him upward and inward, like material gravity pulling objects to their source, so does spiritual gravity pull our personality-selves towards its source. Those who resist this spiritual "pull," seem to be in a free-fall without direction - free from the burden of responsibility of having to act accordingly, only then to be enslaved by random cause and effect, while those who allow themselves to be drawn to a spiritual purpose take on the task of pursuing truth wherever it may lead them, exhausting and unsure as it may be, but rewarding and fulfilling it is!

It is written, "Be you perfect, even as I am perfect," and this is the running theme throughout the Revelation, that we are all children of a living, loving Creator, not one who watches over us waiting for the next mistake, but rather, a guiding spirit that joins in our own effort to find our way through the maze of life.

We struggle, but when downcast, are uplifted by some strange feeling that we are not alone. Even on the most basic level a simple cell seeks to heal when damaged, a cut heals, and even motion seeks equilibrium. All living things strive for perfection, nature strives for balance; man strives to be content.

The drive to progress and to be perfect seems to me proof that the universe is divinely inspired.

The desire for perfection *is the driving force in reality.*

17 FINAL THOUGHTS ON THE REVELATION

The first sentence in the Revelation reads:

"The Universal Father is the God of all creation, the First Source and Center of all things and beings. First think of God as a creator, then as a controller, and lastly as an infinite upholder."

The last sentence on page 2,097 of the Revelation reads:

And all these things are a part of the Universal Father. The Father is living love, and this life of the Father is in his Sons. And the spirit of the Father is in his Sons' sons--mortal men. When all is said and done, the Father idea is still the highest human concept of God.

The single recurring theme of the papers is the very truth that God is the beginning and the end. But the concept of a personal God is, for many, very difficult to believe. How could an infinite Creator of all things be something as simple as a personality?

Perhaps the success of Jesus' appeal to those who follow him is because *he is an approachable personality.*

A personal relationship with an infinite Creator, the same kind of relationship you might have with a spouse, close friend or sibling, is hard to imagine, and yet, the Revelators state very clearly that this relationship is *absolutely attainable.* Having a one-on-one inner relationship with the Universal Father *is* a reality because of one very important element: God is personal, he is the source of all personality, and he is a part of every personality in existence. This is the miracle.

While it may be easy to believe in the *fact* of a 'higher power,' or a force, it's much more difficult to conceive of a loving, father-child relationship with something perceived by the mind as force. Force is not personal; a *Father* is.

Just as Christianity has made the focus of their religion on the risen Christ (instead of the more personable human Jesus), so has modern religion become a theology based on the rule of a Law rather than a personal, loving Creator who actually participates with us as we struggle through our daily life.

To Christians it may be sufficient to have a relationship with Jesus, and he does transform, but Jesus himself repeatedly told his followers to *seek the Father*. His life is an example of what happens when a child *trusts his Father*.

Regardless of whether we acknowledge him as a personality, God still acknowledges us by agreeing to live within each and every personality in the far-flung universe. This concept of unconditional love seems to evade almost all religions because the emphasis of religious living has more to do with performing an act instead of accepting a simple truth that we are all, without condition, part of a cosmic family, with God at the head of the table. The God of a far-flung and vast universe is more than a stern law-giver or Infinite Judge. The Father concept calls on all personalities to view themselves as spiritual children; neither are we servant nor slave. We are physical in appearance, we are intellectual in our design and we are *spiritual* because a fragment of the Father's spirit *lives in us*.

The Revelators desire was to provide modern man with an up-to-date spiritual concept that is both philosophically, scientifically and religiously consistent. This is not to say that the Bible or any other spiritual document is outdated, for truthful concepts remain ever so, but the Revelators wanted to provide more clarification as to our historical origins, as well as our purpose and our spiritual destiny as human beings. They chose to provide a panoramic overview of information that would give us a glimpse of what is to come for all of us once we leave this material estate. Equally as important, they chose to provide us with a better understanding of ourselves so that we could make the most of the world in which we now live. The authors wanted to reveal something of how the universe operates, who inhabits it and how it is administered.

Our early history suggests that on many occasions, periodic revelation had been given to man. Folk tales of giants and mysterious visitors are found in almost every culture and religion. It is not so preposterous to suggest that perhaps those early legends had their basis in some real occurrence that, as the Revelators clearly say, did occur when man was taking his first baby steps long ago. Revelation has come in many forms over eons of time, always appearing in a format *best suited for the time at hand*, usually spiritually illuminated by a prophet or figurehead who was told something new from "the other side."

It is not so hard to believe that, in this modern day of technology, perhaps the only means available by which to provide man with a new Revelation about his origins, destiny and purpose was in book form. The Revelators say they did not want to have any human association with this Revelation *in order to avoid the starting of another religion*. Even the identity of the person who was the original contact with Dr. Sadler during the early years of communication in the 1920's remained a secret. Only the book remains.

It may have been in the Revelators best judgment to provide a new revelation of truth in book form. In this way, the individual is left free to decide whether to accept it as authentic or not. In this way there could be no human influence which would alter or influence human interpretation, as many Revelations have been misinterpreted in the past. No institution will control The Urantia Book, it is open to everyone to discover, and if it accomplishes the mission of bringing men closer to a personal God, then it will have succeeded.

Hundreds of thousands of people have embraced the book as authentic because they have poured over her pages for long periods of time and sense the truth of what is being stated.

Some have looked for inconsistencies but have found few or none. Others discard it because it challenges one to accept concepts that seem too unorthodox, while still many more have stated that the Revelation only confirms what they suspected all along, that our universe is more than solar orbs spinning endlessly without purpose, and that our existence is actually very lovingly organized and full of real purpose. What's more, we are all participants. We are all a part of its continued growth.

The panorama portrayed on its pages inspires one to believe the future is very exciting indeed, for we will all have the opportunity to be a part of its progress.

But even revealed truth has its limitations. The authors say truth is relative and partial - limited only by the age and time in which it is presented. While the truth of God is absolute, eternal, infinite and the source of that very truth, our understanding of him must evolve as we evolve in spiritual understanding and in receptivity:

"The Urantia Papers. The papers, of which this is one, constitute the most recent presentation of truth to the mortals of Urantia. These papers differ from all previous revelations, for they are not the work of a single universe personality but a composite presentation by many beings. But no revelation short of the attainment of the Universal Father can ever be complete. All other celestial ministrations are no more than partial, transient, and practically adapted to local conditions in time and space. While such admissions as this may possibly detract from the immediate force and authority of all revelations, the time has arrived on Urantia when it is advisable to make such frank statements, even at the risk of weakening the future influence and authority of this, the most recent of the revelations of truth to the mortal races of Urantia."

18 CONCLUSIONS AND ORIGINAL CONCEPTS

So I have taken you on a rather long and sometimes complicated journey through the world as it is portrayed by supposed celestial beings on the pages of the Urantia Book.

Dr. Sadler, in addressing early criticism from those who felt the Urantia Book was unoriginal or offered nothing new to theology, offered sixty-four concepts that he believed were and are both unique and original with the Urantia Papers.

In looking over these points, consider the vast scope of subject matter contained within its 2,097 pages and the effort it would have taken to pull something like this off – and sustain credibility while doing so.

Even if one discards the Urantia Book as incredulous or fictional, one still has to appreciate the wide array of subject matter contained therein.

Said Dr. Sadler:

"I submit sixty-four concepts and doctrines which are new and original as presented in The Urantia Book, not to mention more than one hundred additional narratives which represent enlargement, amplification, and clarification of existing knowledge:

1. *The Eternal Son of Paradise: For the first time in human records clearly designated and personally identified.*
2. *The unique Conjoint Actor: The concept of the Third Person of Deity is both unique and original in the Urantia Papers.*
3. *The Paradise Trinity: In The Urantia Book the Paradise Trinity finds its only present-day identification and recognition.*
4. *The Central Geographic Residence of Deity: For the first time the world knows exactly where God lives.*
5. *The absolute Isle of Paradise: The original concept of Paradise as the absolute of non-deity reality.*
6. *Multiple Creator Sons: Recognition of more than 700,000 Creator Paradise Sons.*
7. *Concept of the Absolutes: The concept of the Unqualified, Universal, and Deity Absolutes is original with the Urantia Book.*
8. *Doctrine of Evolutionary Deity: While I saw an intimation of finite Deity in one of Pratt's books about the time of the coming of the Urantia Papers, I am sure that the concepts of the Supreme Being and God the Ultimate are original.*
9. *Concept of the Triunities: The Triunities are an original Urantia concept.*
10. *Havona Universe and Natives: The billion world picture of Havona and its inhabitants is a wholly new and original concept.*
11. *The Concept of Space: Notwithstanding the theory of an "exploding cosmos," the space concept of The Urantia Book is new and original.*
12. *The Grand and Master Universes: The overall concept of the Master cosmos is not only original, but it far transcends all previous ideas.*
13. *The Seven Orders of Trinity-Created Days: While one of these seven orders, the "Ancients of Days," is mentioned in the Bible, the whole presentation is both new and original.*
14. *The Paradise Sons of God: The story of Magisterial and Trinity Teacher Sons in addition to Creator Sons is entirely original with The Urantia Book.*
15. *Trinitized Sons of God: The story and technique of the trinitization of divine Sons is unique and original in the Urantia Papers.*

16. *The Seven Master Spirits: While the Bible makes mention of seven Spirits of God, it is only in The Urantia Book that these Spirits are identified and their work fully described.*

17. *The Vast Family of the Conjoint Actor: The vast and far-flung family of the Infinite Spirit: Supernaphim, Seconaphim, Solitary Messengers are but briefly foreshadowed by the Biblical narrative of seraphim and cherubim.*

18. *The Universal Circuits: The gravity, personality, spirit, and mind circuits are original teaching of The Urantia Book.*

19. *Universal Reflectivity - Majeston: The amazing story of universal reflectivity is a wholly new an original presentation of the Urantia revelation.*

20. *Power Directors- Force Organizers: The whole concept of intelligent and purposive control of cosmic energy is original with The Urantia Book.*

21. *Evolution of Energy - Matter: While some phases of the Urantia story of the evolution of energy may have been foreshadowed by scientific discovery, nevertheless, the concept as a whole is new as presented in the Urantia Papers.*

22. *The Ultimaton: At the time of the suggestion of the Ultimaton in the Urantia Papers, I had never heard of such a concept in scientific literature. During the past five or six years, I have noted several different intimations of the possible existence of some physical factor analogous to the ultimaton concept.*

23. *Origin of the Solar System: While the Urantia narrative of the origin of the solar system includes some features of the Moulton-Chamberlain theory, the whole story is so complete and unique as to make it practically an original presentation.*

24. *The Architectural Worlds: Worlds made to order of specifications is original with The Urantia Book.*

25. *Universe Administration: From the inhabited world to the management of the grand universe the administrative scheme of The Urantia Book is entirely new.*

26. *The Life Carriers: Nothing like the concept of the Life Carriers has ever been suggested to humankind in all past history*

27. *Origin of the Human Race:* While the Urantia story of the origin of the human race validates doctrine of evolution, nevertheless, it presents such a detailed and unique narrative as to constitute an all but original presentation of human origins.

28. *Origin of the Colored Races:* The Urantia story of the origin of the Sangik races is the only such narrative in existence.

29. *Source and Nature of Personality:* While the Urantia Book, like science, fails to define personality, it does designate its origin and gratifyingly portrays its magnificent destiny.

30. *The Concept of Thought Adjusters:* While the Bible talks about the "true light which lighteth every man coming into the world," the story of Thought Adjusters as revealed in the Urantia Papers is so replete and unique as to constitute a new and original story.

31. *Evolution of the Soul:* The concept of the origin, nature, and evolution of the soul is original with The Urantia Book.

32. *Identification of the Holy Spirit:* Pointing out the Holy Spirit as the presence of the Local Universe Mother Spirit is altogether new and original in the Urantia Papers.

33. *The Seven Adjutant Spirits:* While the Bible makes mention of seven spirits and in Isaiah partially identifies them, the Urantia narrative is so full and unique as to make it an original presentation.

34. *Local Universe Sons of God:* The whole story of Local Universe Sons is new and original.

35. *The Ascension Plan þ Be You Perfect:* While Jesus propounded the mandate "Be you perfect," etc., the unfoldment of the Paradise ascension plan in The Urantia Book is an all but new and original concept.

36. *The Seven Mansion Worlds:* While the Master alluded to the "mansion worlds," the replete story of their nature and province is both new and original.

37. *The Morontia Concept:* The whole morontia concept the stage between the material and the spiritual is new and original.

38. *Celestial Artisans and Reversion Directors:* Both of these concepts are new in The Urantia Book. The concept of celestial play and spiritual humor is all but new.

39. *Concept of Permanent Citizenship:* This is wholly original with The Urantia Book.

40. *The Urantia Midwayers: While the Old Testament does refer to the "Nephilim" the citation is so indefinite as to constitute the Urantia story of the midwayers as a new and original narrative.*

41. *The Superhuman Planetary Government: The story of the planetary functions of the Most Highs, the Reserve Corps, and the planetary seraphim is original, notwithstanding the allusion to the work of the Most Highs in the Bible.*

42. *The Billions of Inhabited Worlds: At the time of the arrival of the Urantia Papers, there was no literature dealing with inhabited worlds other than our world. The idea was new. In recent years we frequently run across speculations regarding other inhabited planets.*

43. *Clarification of Sin and Rebellion: The unique clarification of sin and rebellion is original with The Urantia Book.*

44. *Identification of Adam and Eve: The factual narrative of the legendary story of Adam and Eve is original.*

45. *Clarification of Melchizedek: The Melchizedek story as clarified in the Urantia narrative is really a new and original concept.*

46. *Concept of the Ages of Light and Life: The fruition of mortal evolution as portrayed in the concept of the ages of light and life is altogether new and original.*

47. *A Unified History of Urantia: Nowhere else in all the world can you find a consistent and unified history of our world. For the first time we have a chronology of human affairs.*

48. *Diseases: The Book presents a new and original explanation of microbic diseases.*

49. *Antigravity: The whole concept of antigravity-is unique and original with the Urantia Papers. Only during the last year has any scientist promulgated a theory of antigravity.*

50. *Jesus' Birthday: For the first time during the Christian era, we know the real birthday of Jesus--August 21, 7BC.*

51. *Experimental Planet: The fact that Urantia was a decimal planet that the Life Carriers had permission to attempt new features of biologic evolution. This is information not heretofore known on the planet.*

52. *The Evolution of Religion: While you can read much about the evolution of religion on Urantia, nevertheless, the straightforward story told in the Urantia Papers is unique and original.*

53. *The Unique Reason for Jesus' Bestowal: The Urantia Book presents a new, unique, and original reason for Jesus' life and death on our world.*

54. *A Chronological Story of Jesus' Life: The Book presents the only complete story of Jesus' life on this world.*

55. *Identification of the Twelve Apostles: The Urantia story is the first time the confusion of the 12 Apostles has been straightened out.*

56. *The Unique Story of Mary: The story of Mary, the mother of Jesus, is unique and original.*

57. *The Water and the Wine: As far as I know, The Urantia Book presents an original explanation of this supposed miracle.*

58. *Explanation of Unintended Miracles: The Book presents a possible explanation of numerous unintended miracles.*

59. *Jesus' Attitude toward Art and Athletics: The Master's attitude toward art and athletics is nowhere else revealed.*

60. *The Sermon on the Mount: I am, of course, not familiar with all the literature on the Sermon on the Mount. But as far as I know, the interpretation of this address in The Urantia Book is new and original.*

61. *The Women's Evangelistic Corps: This story is new, notwithstanding the brief mention of this matter in the New Testament.*

62. *Rodan of Alexandria: This whole story is original with The Urantia Book.*

63. *The Story of Abner: The unique story of the head of John the Baptist's apostles is original with the Urantia Papers.*

64. *David Zebedee' s Intelligence Corps: This entire story is exclusively Found in The Urantia Book*

Dr. Sadler was perhaps one of the most critical and skeptical thinkers of his day, certainly one who had dedicated his life to science and earnest knowledge. His sixty-four examples of the original and unique concepts "presented for the first time" in the Urantia Book are worthy of intense scholarly debate and examination, and should intrigue future readers from all fields of study for years and decades to come.

If one loves religion, theology, history, astronomy, philosophy or even physics, one cannot help to recognize and appreciate the enormous task that was undertaken by those who wrote the Urantia Book.

And is there any literature in existence right now that attempts to explain so much with such great detail and with such incredible consistency?

Is there any religion, faith or belief system that dares to address and explain the nature and personality of God, angels, spiritual existence, life after death, the evolution of living systems (both here and in the physical universe), life on other worlds, man's early history, the soul, Jesus's day-by-day life, historical and sociological evolution, the origins and destiny of man, the geological beginnings of our earth, our solar system, our physical universe, and the very purpose of life itself?

When I first began reading the Urantia Book I was conflicted because I wanted to believe it was true – if only because it did seem to explain a lot of missing links in our history, and it really did present a seemingly logical explanation of how life is set up in the universe.

Even so, it is hard to swallow that someone could know such things. It took years for me to critically evaluate whether what the book was saying could be logical and feasible. I am a skeptic at heart, one not easily fooled. And I can attest that through the years I have carefully studied the book and have observed who is attracted to it, always looking for a flaw. I understand why so many people reject it. They reject it because it is too good to be true. It is too hard to fathom that someone could know such things about reality. But there is one passage in the book that has always stuck with me, as it seemed to speak to me and beckoned me not to give up my earnest search as to whether this Urantia Book could be a revelation of new truth, as it claims to be.

I have always believed in God, so my faith was never based on whether the Urantia Book was true or not. My faith is based on my own personal experience of feeling the spirit within me. All the Urantia Book has done for me (and presumably others) is confirm what I already believed in anyway. But with regard for searching for the truth – and being willing to follow it wherever it may lead – consider what Jesus said about having the courage to follow the truth:

From page 1730, (Paper 155, Section 6) Jesus said:

"You have come out from among those of your fellows who choose to remain satisfied with a religion of mind, who crave security and prefer conformity. You have elected to exchange your feelings of authoritative certainty for the assurances of the spirit of adventurous and progressive faith. You have dared to protest against the grueling bondage of institutional religion and to reject the authority of the traditions of record which are now regarded as the word of God. Our Father did indeed speak through Moses, Elijah, Isaiah, Amos, and Hosea, but he did not cease to minister words of truth to the world when these prophets of old made an end of their utterances. My Father is no respecter of races or generations in that the word of truth is vouchsafed one age and withheld from another. Commit not the folly of calling that divine which is wholly human, and fail not to discern the words of truth which come not through the traditional oracles of supposed inspiration.

"I have called upon you to be born again, to be born of the spirit. I have called you out of the darkness of authority and the lethargy of tradition into the transcendent light of the realization of the possibility of making for yourselves the greatest discovery possible for the human soul to make — the supernal experience of finding God for yourself, in yourself, and of yourself, and of doing all this as a fact in your own personal experience. And so may you pass from death to life, from the authority of tradition to the experience of knowing God; thus will you pass from darkness to light, from a racial faith inherited to a personal faith achieved by actual experience; and thereby will you progress from a theology of mind handed down by your ancestors to a true religion of spirit which shall be built up in your souls as an eternal endowment.

"Your religion shall change from the mere intellectual belief in traditional authority to the actual experience of that living faith

which is able to grasp the reality of God and all that relates to the divine spirit of the Father. The religion of the mind ties you hopelessly to the past; the religion of the spirit consists in progressive revelation and ever beckons you on toward higher and holier achievements in spiritual ideals and eternal realities.

"While the religion of authority may impart a present feeling of settled security, you pay for such a transient satisfaction the price of the loss of your spiritual freedom and religious liberty. My Father does not require of you as the price of entering the kingdom of heaven that you should force yourself to subscribe to a belief in things which are spiritually repugnant, unholy, and untruthful. It is not required of you that your own sense of mercy, justice, and truth should be outraged by submission to an outworn system of religious forms and ceremonies. The religion of the spirit leaves you forever free to follow the truth wherever the leadings of the spirit may take you. And who can judge — perhaps this spirit may have something to impart to this generation which other generations have refused to hear?

"Shame on those false religious teachers who would drag hungry souls back into the dim and distant past and there leave them! And so are these unfortunate persons doomed to become frightened by every new discovery, while they are discomfited by every new revelation of truth. The prophet who said, "He will be kept in perfect peace whose mind is stayed on God," was not a mere intellectual believer in authoritative theology. This truth-knowing human had discovered God; he was not merely talking about God.

"I admonish you to give up the practice of always quoting the prophets of old and praising the heroes of Israel, and instead aspire to become living prophets of the Most High and spiritual heroes of the coming kingdom. To honor the God-knowing leaders of the past may indeed be worthwhile, but why, in so doing, should you sacrifice the supreme experience of human existence: finding God for yourselves and knowing him in your own souls?

"Every race of mankind has its own mental outlook upon human existence; therefore must the religion of the mind ever run true to these various racial viewpoints. Never can the religions of authority come to unification. Human unity and mortal brotherhood can be achieved only by and through the super endowment of the religion of the spirit. Racial minds may differ, but all mankind is indwelt by the same divine and eternal spirit. The hope of human brotherhood can only be realized when, and as, the divergent mind religions of authority become impregnated with, and overshadowed by, the unifying and ennobling religion of the spirit — the religion of personal spiritual experience.

"The religions of authority can only divide men and set them in conscientious array against each other; the religion of the spirit will progressively draw men together and cause them to become understandingly sympathetic with one another. The religions of authority require of men uniformity in belief, but this is impossible of realization in the present state of the world. The religion of the spirit requires only unity of experience — uniformity of destiny — making full allowance for diversity of belief. The religion of the spirit requires only uniformity of insight, not uniformity of viewpoint and outlook. The religion of the spirit does not demand uniformity of intellectual views, only unity of spirit feeling. The religions of authority crystallize into lifeless creeds; the religion of the spirit grows into the increasing joy and liberty of ennobling deeds of loving service and merciful ministration.

"But watch, lest any of you look with disdain upon the children of Abraham because they have fallen on these evil days of traditional barrenness. Our forefathers gave themselves up to the persistent and passionate search for God, and they found him as no other whole race of men have ever known him since the times of Adam, who knew much of this as he was himself a Son of God. My Father has not failed to mark the long and untiring struggle of Israel, ever since the days of Moses, to find God and to know God. For weary generations the Jews have not ceased to toil, sweat, groan, travail, and endure the sufferings and experience the sorrows of a misunderstood and despised people, all in order that

they might come a little nearer the discovery of the truth about God. And, notwithstanding all the failures and falterings of Israel, our fathers progressively, from Moses to the times of Amos and Hosea, did reveal increasingly to the whole world an ever clearer and more truthful picture of the eternal God. And so was the way prepared for the still greater revelation of the Father which you have been called to share.

"Never forget there is only one adventure which is more satisfying and thrilling than the attempt to discover the will of the living God, and that is the supreme experience of honestly trying to do that divine will. And fail not to remember that the will of God can be done in any earthly occupation. Some callings are not holy and others secular. All things are sacred in the lives of those who are spirit led; that is, subordinated to truth, ennobled by love, dominated by mercy, and restrained by fairness — justice. The spirit which my Father and I shall send into the world is not only the Spirit of Truth but also the spirit of idealistic beauty.

"You must cease to seek for the word of God only on the pages of the olden records of theologic authority. Those who are born of the spirit of God shall henceforth discern the word of God regardless of whence it appears to take origin. Divine truth must not be discounted because the channel of its bestowal is apparently human. Many of your brethren have minds which accept the theory of God while they spiritually fail to realize the presence of God. And that is just the reason why I have so often taught you that the kingdom of heaven can best be realized by acquiring the spiritual attitude of a sincere child. It is not the mental immaturity of the child that I commend to you but rather the spiritual simplicity of such an easy-believing and fully-trusting little one. It is not so important that you should know about the fact of God as that you should increasingly grow in the ability to feel the presence of God.

"When you once begin to find God in your soul, presently you will begin to discover him in other men's souls and eventually in all the creatures and creations of a mighty universe. But what chance

does the Father have to appear as a God of supreme loyalties and divine ideals in the souls of men who give little or no time to the thoughtful contemplation of such eternal realities? While the mind is not the seat of the spiritual nature, it is indeed the gateway thereto. "But do not make the mistake of trying to prove to other men that you have found God; you cannot consciously produce such valid proof, albeit there are two positive and powerful demonstrations of the fact that you are God-knowing, and they are: 1. The fruits of the spirit of God showing forth in your daily routine life. 2. The fact that your entire life plan furnishes positive proof that you have unreservedly risked everything you are and have on the adventure of survival after death in the pursuit of the hope of finding the God of eternity, whose presence you have foretasted in time.

Now, mistake not, my Father will ever respond to the faintest flicker of faith. He takes note of the physical and superstitious emotions of the primitive man. And with those honest but fearful souls whose faith is so weak that it amounts to little more than an intellectual conformity to a passive attitude of assent to religions of authority, the Father is ever alert to honor and foster even all such feeble attempts to reach out for him. But you who have been called out of darkness into the light are expected to believe with a whole heart; your faith shall dominate the combined attitudes of body, mind, and spirit. You are my apostles, and to you religion shall not become a theologic shelter to which you may flee in fear of facing the rugged realities of spiritual progress and idealistic adventure; but rather shall your religion become the fact of real xperience which testifies that God has found you, idealized, ennobled, and spiritualized you, and that you have enlisted in the eternal adventure of finding the God who has thus found and sonshipped you.

"And when Jesus had finished speaking, he beckoned to Andrew and, pointing to the west toward Phoenicia, said: "Let us be on our way."